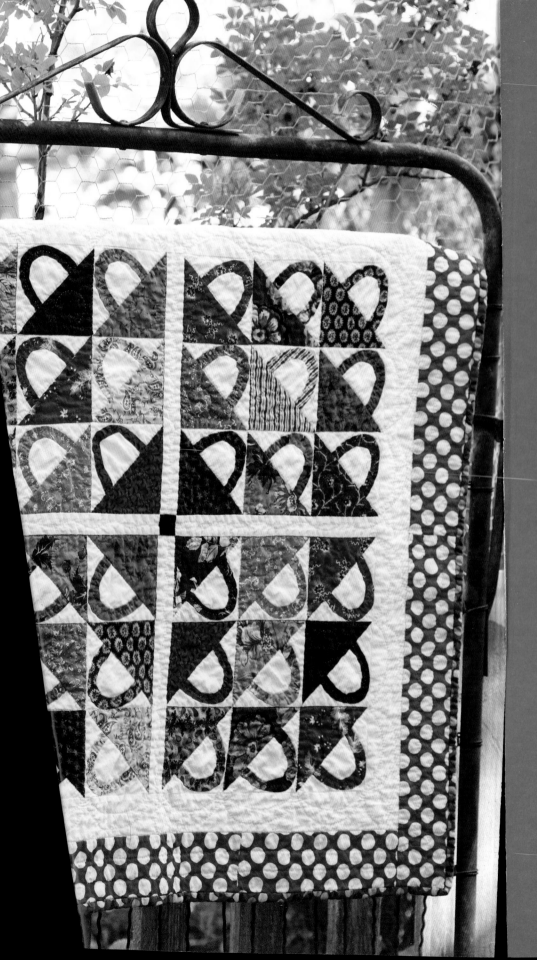

Hand-Appliquéd Quilts

Whimsical Designs & Simple Techniques

TONYE BELINDA PHILLIPS

LARK BOOKS

A Division of Sterling Publishing Co., Inc.
New York / London

Red Lips 4 Courage Communications, Inc.

www.redlips4courage.com

Eileen Cannon Paulin
President

Catherine Risling
Director of Editorial

Book Editor: Rebecca Ittner
Copy Editors: Cathy Risling, Darra Williamson
Book Design: Rose Sheifer-Wright
Photographer: Zac Williams

Library of Congress Cataloging-in-Publication Data

Library of Congress Cataloging-in-Publication Data

Phillips, Tonye Belinda.
 Hand-appliquéd quilts whimsical designs & simple techniques / Tonye Belinda Phillips. -- 1st ed.
    p. cm.
 Includes index.

ISBN-13: 978-1-60059-254-6 (hc-plc with jacket : alk. paper)
ISBN-10: 1-60059-254-6 (hc-plc with jacket : alk. paper)
1. Appliqué--Patterns. 2. Quilting--Patterns. I. Title.
TT779.P49135 2008
746.44'5041--dc22

                                        2007041116

First Edition
Published by Lark Books, A Division of
Sterling Publishing Co., Inc.
387 Park Avenue South, New York, NY 10016

Text © 2008, Tonye Belinda Phillips
Photography © 2008, Red Lips 4 Courage Communications, Inc.
Illustrations © 2008, Red Lips 4 Courage Communications, Inc.

Distributed in Canada by Sterling Publishing,
c/o Canadian Manda Group, 165 Dufferin Street
Toronto, Ontario, Canada M6K 3H6

Distributed in the United Kingdom by GMC Distribution Services,
Castle Place, 166 High Street, Lewes, East Sussex, England BN7 1XU
Distributed in Australia by Capricorn Link (Australia) Pty Ltd.,
P.O. Box 704, Windsor, NSW 2756 Australia

If you have questions or comments about this book, please contact:
Lark Books
67 Broadway
Asheville, NC 28801
(828) 253-0467

Manufactured in China

ISBN 10: 1-60059-254-6

ISBN 13: 978-1-60059-254-6

For information about custom editions, special sales, premium and corporate
purchases, please contact Sterling Special Sales Department at (800) 805-5489
or specialsales@sterlingpub.com.

Dedication

I dedicate this book, my
very first, to my incredibly
supportive, creative, smart,
and clever husband, Doug,
and to our fantastic boys,
Ande and Charlie. They are
the reason I am able to do
what I love to do.

CONTENTS

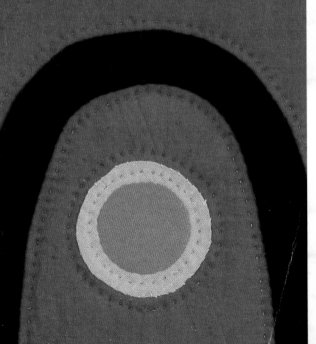

INTRODUCTION

For the Love of Appliqué

Several years ago, while laid up with a skiing injury, I was faced with spending a considerable amount of time on the sofa. I am not very good at lying around, so I *had* to spend this forced period of convalescence *doing* something. At the same time, I had just begun using hand appliqué in my quilts, so I seized the opportunity to dive into my new obsession, and I haven't stopped since.

Having a bright and colorful quilt to work on every day is my salvation. Hand appliqué is like meditation to me; it gives me much-needed time to sit, reflect, and relax during and after a hectic day. In this busy world, I feel it is important to carve out a bit of downtime every day. I love that appliqué can be done in total silence, or while watching a favorite movie or listening to a good book on tape—whatever suits my mood on any given day.

In this book, I will take you into a favorite part of my life and share the simplified, no-fuss way I hand-appliqué my quilts. I believe that there is no "right way" or "wrong way" to create a quilt. I just make them *my* way. It is my goal to provide the information necessary for you to feel comfortable creating hand-appliquéd, folk-art-style quilts—*your* way. To get you started, I will teach you basic appliqué techniques, and share tips and tricks I have discovered throughout my years of quilting.

On the following pages, you'll find that this book is not about achieving appliqué perfection; it is about getting started with simple shapes and simple design. Appliqué adds so much interest to quilt designs. Once you get the hang of it, your skill will progress with each stitch, and I promise you will get better and faster. As you will discover, my technique is really a basic "get-out-there-and-do-it" kind of appliqué.

Along with appliqué templates, I have provided detailed instructions for each quilt. It is my hope that you will pick and choose some of the elements that appeal to you—an interesting shape or a colorful, whimsical fabric—and then incorporate them into your quilt. I truly believe that we all have an intuitive design sense. We know what we like and how it makes us feel.

Many years of knitting, cross-stitch, and crewel embroidery got me hooked on handwork. A book about primitive folk-art appliqué sparked my initial interest in quilting. My family and I live in a very rustic, woodsy setting, and when I spotted this book, it struck a chord. Even though my designs have evolved, and my color choices keep getting brighter and brighter, I will always love quilts with a vintage, folk-art, naive look and feel. I am drawn to quilts that are a little bit odd, in a charming sort of way. Much of my inspiration comes from quirky, goofy quilts. There is nothing that delights me more than a quilt that presents the unexpected.

The quilts featured in this book are all inspired by what I love. We have several window boxes on our cottage and cabin/studio, and they served as the inspiration for my *Window Box* quilt (page 40). (Of course, this quilt represents what I really want my flowers to

look like.) *Heirloom Roses* (page 45) was inspired by the beautiful rose catalogs we receive every spring. We can't grow roses like these in our area, but now I can look at this quilt all year and dream. *Viva Mexico* (page 50) was created from the memories of an amazing year my husband and I and our two boys spent sailing our boat from Oregon down the West Coast and through Mexico.

The satisfaction that I get from hand appliqué is difficult to describe. The sense of accomplishment and of learning a time-tested skill is a wonderful thing. If teaching you these techniques can do just a little bit to keep this tradition alive,

we together will have accomplished a lot. It is important to honor our past; to remember those who came before us and passed on their expertise, their creativity, and their love.

Now you need to give yourself permission to go for it! May reading this book be a delightful journey for you, and one that inspires you to get started on a hand-appliquéd quilt of your own. Have fun!

tonye belinda phillips

CHAPTER ONE

GETTING STARTED

Simply through the act of creating, every quilt artist develops a list of preferred tools, fabrics, and color choices. In this chapter you will find my essentials, as well as information to help you choose colors and fabrics for your quilts. I will also share my ideas about quilt design.

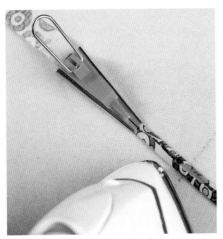
Bias tape makers provide a simple way to make stems and vines.

Cutting mats and acrylic rulers are must-haves for every quilter. Keep a range of sizes on hand. A swivel mat is especially handy for squaring and cutting small pieces.

Tools of the Trade

The appliqué process I use is fairly simple, but there are some basic items that will help you stitch like a pro sooner rather than later. Before starting any project in this book, equip your space with the necessary tools and supplies, and make sure you have a large work surface and adequate lighting.

BATTING

As with just about everything related to quilting, there are many different choices for batting. My preference for the last several years has been 100-percent cotton batting. I prefer a very thin batting that is easy to stitch by hand. This type of batting makes a very soft and supple quilt with an old-fashioned look and feel.

My advice is to study quilts that you like and, if possible, find out which type of batting the maker used. Your local quilt shop has information about batting and you can research online as well. Some batting is better for wall hangings, while others are ideal for bed quilts. Whether a quilt will be machine quilted or hand quilted will also make a difference in your choice of batting. The best

way to decide what type of batting works best for your quilts is through researching and then trying different options.

BIAS TAPE MAKER

A bias tape maker lets you create bias tape from cotton quilting fabric—perfect to use for vines and stems. I use ¼" (.6 mm) and ½" (1.3 cm) bias tape makers when creating my quilts. These tools also come in larger sizes.

CUTTING MAT

I use cutting mats in a variety of sizes, depending on the area of my available workspace. A larger mat is essential on a permanent cutting surface. The smaller sizes are handy next to my machine and for use when I am traveling. I also use a small swivel model for cutting around blocks and small pieces without having to pick up and move the fabric.

FREEZER PAPER

Freezer paper is used to create iron-on templates, and is available at grocery stores, quilt shops, and online.

IRON

When selecting an iron for quilt work, be sure to choose one that can be adjusted to a cotton setting with steam.

MARKING TOOLS

There are many different types of marking tools available. For light fabrics I use a #2 lead pencil, and for dark fabrics I use chalk pencils in different colors.

NEEDLES AND PINS

Like all quilters, I have my favorite types and sizes of needles and pins. Sizes vary widely between manufacturers, so you'll want to experiment with different brands to find what works best for you.

For the hand-appliqué process, my favorite needles are size #11 straw needles. They are long and quite thin, and barely leave a mark on the fabric. I also use size #11 milliners needles.

To hand quilt, I use #9 or #10 between quilting needles. Quilting needles are very short; the higher the number, the smaller the needle.

Make sure to keep a variety of sizes of pins and needles on hand for different fabric weights and tasks. Thimbles ensure a safe, enjoyable appliqué experience.

Note: The eyes of appliqué and quilting needles can be quite small. Using a needle threader will ease any frustration when threading needles.

I use basting needles when thread-basting my quilts. These long, thin needles are designed to go through multiple quilt layers easily.

When doing appliqué, I use appliqué pins for basting. These thin pins do not leave a noticeable mark in fabric. I prefer the glass-head variety, in 36mm and 48mm lengths.

Keep a variety of pin styles and sizes on hand to use with different fabric weights, as well as for different tasks such as pinning quilts to a design wall.

QUILTING FRAMES AND HOOPS

Quilting frames and hoops come in a wide variety of shapes and sizes, and are used to hold quilt layers together for hand quilting. I use a 14" (35.6 cm) wooden hoop when quilting my work.

ROTARY CUTTERS

Used along with a cutting mat, a rotary cutter allows you to make multiple straight cuts safely and accurately. I use a standard 45mm blade. To ensure accuracy of cuts and prevent frustration, always work with a sharp blade.

RULERS

Clear acrylic quilter's rulers make it easy to measure blocks and square them to size. Clear rulers come with markings in a variety of colors; choose one with easy-to-see measurements. I use 6" x 12" (15.2 x 30.5 cm), 3" x 18" (7.6 x 45.7 cm), and 12" x 24" (30.5 x 61 cm) sizes most often

SCISSORS

I have an arsenal of scissors at my disposal when creating my quilts. Fabric and craft scissors (for cutting paper and template material) are absolute necessities. I also have a quality pair of small, sharp embroidery scissors on hand for cutting out appliqué pieces and for snipping "curves and valleys" and loose threads.

SEAM RIPPER

Unfortunately, no quilter can be without one of these. A good-quality seam ripper allows the easy removal of stitches and minimizes damage to fabric.

SEWING MACHINE

The projects in this book require a sewing machine that can do a reliable straight stitch. My 25-year-old Viking Husqvarna sewing machine was a wedding gift from my mother-in-law. Though it has a variety of attachments, I have never used them. The machine sews a nice straight line, and that is all I need.

THIMBLES

A thimble protects your finger as you work the needle through layers of fabric, making hand appliqué and hand quilting a safe and enjoyable experience. I fought wearing one when I first learned to quilt, but now I can't quilt without one.

Find a quilting thimble that fits comfortably on the middle finger of the hand you sew with. The thimble should be snug, but not too tight. I keep a few sizes on hand, so no matter what size my fingers may be on a given day, I always have a thimble that fits. Though I use and recommend metal thimbles, a wide variety of thimble styles are available, including leather, metal, and plastic.

THREAD

When sewing appliqués to the quilt top, use only high-quality 100-percent cotton thread. I use 50 wt. machine thread. For pleasing results, match your thread color to the appliqué piece.

For hand quilting, I use glazed quilting thread. Not only does it glide through multiple layers, but it is also stronger than regular sewing thread. When determining a color for your quilting thread, consider the look you want for your quilt. For a more subtle look, use thread that matches or blends into the background. To accentuate your quilting, use a thread that contrasts with the background.

Any type of thread can be used to baste the layers of your quilt sandwich. I prefer a stiff quilting thread because it won't tangle as I work my way around the quilt.

Choosing Fabric

I am always on the prowl for new fabrics. Quilt shops and fabric stores are chock full of the most enticing colors, prints, patterns, and textures imaginable. When I told my good friend, Marcia, that I had to explain my process for choosing fabric for this book, she looked at me and said, "Well, Tonye, don't you just head straight for the polka dot section and buy as much as you can?" She isn't far off; I've had a thing for polka dots for many years, and now they are more popular and fun than ever. But I do need to be careful that every fabric I own isn't a dot of some sort. It's important to have many *different* fabrics on hand.

When I see a fabric that I just can't take my eyes off of, I'll buy at least three to four yards, and sometimes even five yards. I may end up using it as my "theme" for a quilt, or even as the backing. With other enticing fabrics, I may buy one or two yards, not knowing what role they will play in a later design, but wanting enough to make an impact. In addition, I always buy fat quarters— 18" x 21" (45.7 x 53.3 cm) pieces—or ½ yard (.46 meter) pieces. I won't have a specific plan for them, but this ensures I have enough for basic designs.

In your fabric collection, be sure to include stripes, checks, and bold graphics. These fabrics add a lot of "zing" to quilts and they make good transitional borders. Having a diversified stash of fabric when beginning a new project (or adding to a project) makes the process much more fun. *Note:* Heavyweight or stiff fabrics can be difficult to work with when doing hand appliqué. When choosing fabrics, consider not only color and pattern, but also fabric weight.

I prefer to use 100 percent cotton fabrics.

Fabrics are like magic to me; I love their colors and textures. I invest in a variety of shades of every color so I always have something available to add just the right touch to my quilt.

Don't worry about having enough of any one fabric. If more of the same fabric is unavailable, you will have to push yourself to find something else to make the quilt work. Trust me; it is a great thing to run out of a fabric. View it as an opportunity to get those creative juices flowing. Do not spend a week driving around looking for matching fabric. Instead, dive into your fabric stash, and add the unexpected.

Having Fun With Color

The one comment I hear more than any other about my quilts is that people love the colors. People also tell me that they never would have thought to use a particular fabric in a certain quilt, but that it actually works in my design. My color choices are purely intuitive. I am drawn first to fabrics by their color.

There are many factors that influence my color choices, even my mood when shopping. Some days I choose vintage-inspired fabrics, while other days I select colors that are bright, and maybe even wild. Store displays also influence my selections. Many times a new line of fabric is displayed prominently and I just have to have some of it. I also love the deep, rich, saturated colors that add drama to my designs.

When it comes right down to it, you should use colors that you love. For help in learning what colors work well together, study other quilts. Take notes and use these examples as a guide. You will eventually find your very own style.

When shopping for fabric, be on the lookout for different shades and prints of each color. A wide variety is far more interesting than using the same fabric

throughout a quilt. If one shade of red is good, I think a dozen shades of red are better! Don't be afraid to mix things up. If you feel your design is looking a bit bland, be adventurous. Grab an unusual, contrasting color and see how it looks and feels with your other fabrics.

When designing a quilt, I gather my fabrics and scraps together, lay them out, and study them for a while. I audition a color, and if it doesn't seem to work, I try another. When choosing colors for your quilts, audition different colors together until you are pleased with the results. Don't agonize over or over-analyze your choices; use colors that feel right and make you happy. I get so excited to start on a quilt that I can't be bothered with a lot of over-thinking. Does it get me into trouble sometimes? Yes, but not as often as one might think. For me, this intuitive method keeps the process of creating quilts exciting and enjoyable.

The Design Process

The design of my first appliqué quilt, *Belinda's Baskets* (page 32), was inspired by the containers I saw in vintage quilts, cottage gardens, and in other forms of needlework. Suddenly I saw containers everywhere and just knew they needed to be quilted. This quilt sent me right over the edge, and I haven't stopped appliquéing since.

Design ideas are all around us. Open your eyes to what is right in front of you every day—architecture, window boxes, gardens, needlework, wallpaper, books, and magazines. Studying antique quilts is a favorite pastime of mine, and they are where I turn most often for inspiration. These quilts are fresh, innovative, and often delightfully odd. I attend as many quilt shows as I can to check out quilts up close. Through the years, I have acquired

I love the pieced background I used on *Window Box*. I don't worry too much about the design before I start a quilt because I really enjoy the process and the challenge of using the materials I have on hand.

quite a collection of books, cards, and calendars that chronicle these amazing quilts. I use these resources often for design ideas, interpreting them in my own way in my quilts. Many times I am inspired by a fabric and design the quilt with that fabric in mind.

Once you get into the design mode and start looking around, the ideas will begin to flow and you will find inspiration everywhere. If you are just beginning to appliqué, you will be far more successful if you keep designs simple with fairly large and uncomplicated shapes. With this book, you are designing in the folk-art tradition. Don't get caught up fretting about whether the proportions are correct or the lines are straight. These designs are meant to be playful and fun.

When I am ready to create a new quilt design, I make a very simple sketch of what I have in mind. With this sketch, my main focus is on the center of the quilt, but I will also include a few ideas for borders. This stage is preliminary, and open to as many changes as may be necessary along the way. I prefer not knowing just how the design will play out; I find that this keeps the process much more exciting. When designing your quilts, keep yourself open to change.

Overcoming Design Obstacles

It's so exciting to come up with a new design that I just can't wait to get started. So, I grab what I have and dive in headfirst—not always with a lot of thought as to how it will all go together. Look closely at *Belinda's Baskets* (page 32) and *Window Box* (page 40) and notice how the backgrounds are patched together. In each case, I ran out of the background fabric partway through and had to piece the remaining background. Although I came close to matching the original fabrics, I really like the fact that they are not all the same. This happens in almost all of my quilts. The backgrounds may appear planned, but they really aren't. This is my style of quilting—get started and worry about the details later.

There will be times when you get "stuck" while working on a quilt. You may find that you need to put it away for a while; that is perfectly fine and part of the creative design process. Go on to another idea and come back to the original piece later.

You can find design ideas almost everywhere, from antique quilts to flower boxes. Take these ideas and personalize them in your quilts.

CHAPTER TWO

TECHNIQUES

In this chapter, I will guide you through the methods I use for making appliqué templates and for cutting out appliqué shapes. I will also share my techniques for appliqué and quilting. There are many how-to books on quilt making; if you are new to quilting, you may consider purchasing a good basic guide for reference.

How to Appliqué

Before beginning the appliqué process, cut out a background block or create a pieced background. Basic instructions for backgrounds are included with each project in this book.

STITCHING WISDOM

Preparing the Background

If you are doing a fair amount of appliqué, the background may pull in or shrink up a bit as you stitch. By cutting the background slightly oversized, you will have enough fabric to trim the background to the desired size after you have finished the appliqué process.

MAKING FREEZER-PAPER TEMPLATES

Draw or trace the desired appliqué shapes onto the non-shiny side of freezer paper, making sure to leave space between the shapes so you have room for cutting. (See Fig. 1.) The templates you draw on the freezer paper will be the finished size of your appliqué pieces.

Cut out the freezer-paper templates along the drawn lines. *Note:* Use plastic templates if a design element will be repeated many times.

Fig. 1

USING FREEZER-PAPER TEMPLATES

Iron the shiny side of the freezer-paper template onto the right side of the desired fabric, leaving enough room for a $\frac{1}{4}$" (.6 cm) seam allowance on all sides. It only takes a few seconds to adhere the freezer paper to the fabric. *Note:* I prefer to work from the right side of the fabric so I never need to worry about removing the freezer paper after the piece is sewn to the quilt.

Using a #2 lead pencil or a chalk pencil—whichever shows up best on the fabric—trace around the edge of the template. (See Fig. 2.) This line will be your guide for turning under the seam. *Note: Do not* iron any markings as doing so could make them permanent.

Fig. 2

Cut out the shape leaving a $\frac{1}{4}$" (.6 cm) seam allowance, and remove the template (See Fig. 3.) Make sure you don't cut too small a seam allowance. It is better to have too much fabric, as the excess can be trimmed as you appliqué.

Fig. 3

Note: Templates can be used several times. Discard them when they no longer adhere to the fabric when ironed.

PLACING APPLIQUÉ SHAPES

If you are concerned about centering your appliqué design, fold the background in half both horizontally and vertically, and then from corner to corner in both directions. Press the folded piece to make centering marks. You also can eyeball placement of the appliqué shapes.

Pin the shapes in place on the background. (See Fig. 4.) If you are working with a large appliqué shape, it is best to thread baste the shape in place; pins tend to be cumbersome, and they will poke you as you sew. Whether the shapes are pinned or thread-basted, make sure that the pieces do not end up lopsided, puckered, or lumpy. Continually check as you pin or sew to make sure the shape, big or small, is laying flat.

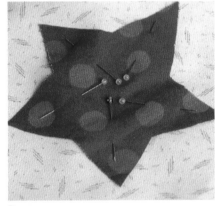

Fig. 4

After you have laid out your design and are happy with the results, take a photograph for reference. Because you will be unpinning the pieces as you work, this photograph is a vital part of the design process. I find it nearly impossible to deal with all those pieces and pins at the same time. It is much easier for me to work on one appliqué shape at a time. Once you have taken a photograph of the design, unpin all but the bottom layer of shapes.

STITCHING APPLIQUÉ SHAPES

Note: I use the invisible needle-turn appliqué stitch when appliquéing a quilt.

When you are ready to appliqué, begin with shapes that will be partially covered by other shapes. For example, when working on a big container quilt, appliqué the container first and leave the top edge open so stems can be inserted later. If there are no stems, finish stitching around the piece and then proceed with remaining shapes.

Using 100-percent cotton thread that matches the color of the appliqué shape, thread a straw or milliners needle with a single 15" (38.1 cm) strand, knotting the end with a quilter's knot. *Note:* A longer strand of thread may tangle or fray after several trips through the fabric.

Use the tip of your needle to turn the seam allowance under along the drawn line. Fold under a 1" (2.5 cm) section,

using the thumb on your non-sewing hand to finger press the seam. (See Fig. 1.) This is an important part of the needle-turn process.

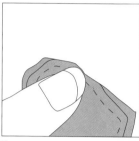
Fig. 1

Start your first stitch with the knot tucked under the appliqué shape. This prevents the thread from showing.

Push the needle through the background fabric so it emerges right next to the appliqué shape, and then come up about ⅛" (.3 cm) ahead, grabbing only a couple of threads on the edge of the appliqué shape. (See Fig. 2.)

Fig. 2

Reinsert the needle into the background fabric right next to the previous stitch, keeping the stitch as close to the appliqué shape as possible without going through the shape. *Note:* If you are new to appliqué, you may find that some of your stitches show if you catch too much fabric, that the edges may not be very smooth, or that some of your stitches may be larger than ⅛" (.3 cm). Don't worry; the quality of your stitches will get better with practice.

Continue in this manner around the entire appliqué shape, using the point and side of the needle to turn the edges under as you go. (See Fig. 3.) Be careful not to pull the thread too tightly as you stitch. You want the appliqué shape to lay flat.

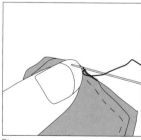
Fig. 3

As you come to the end of the appliqué, stitch about ½" (1.3 cm) beyond the first stitch, and then send the needle through to the background

and knot the thread. Before removing the thread from the needle, send the needle and a tail of thread between the shape and the background to hide the thread, especially on light-colored backgrounds.

Repeat these steps until all of your appliqué shapes are sewn to the background.

Additional Appliqué Techniques

Certain appliqué shapes present challenges to even an experienced quilter. Over the years I have developed my own solutions to these problem shapes. Whether you are dealing with circles or points and valleys, these tried-and-true methods will help you stitch your way to beautiful hand appliqué.

CIRCLES

There are many ways to make circles. Though I am always interested to see what methods others have come up with, I have kept my method simple—just cut out the circles, pin them down, and sew them on. Use the tip of your needle to maneuver the seam allowance into place. You may not like your first attempts, but your circles will get better with practice. Start with big ones; the smaller the shapes, the more difficult they are to handle.

When you cut out a circle, the edges are automatically on the bias. If you decide to clip the edges for further ease in turning, make sure the cuts are evenly spaced. Some experimentation may be necessary to come up with a method that works best for you. Circles are tricky, but keep at it and eventually you will master the technique.

Circles are fun to work with. Though sometimes tough for beginners, these shapes do get easier.

CURVES

As with circles, when you cut a curve in a piece of fabric you have automatically created a bias edge. These edges generally do not need to be clipped unless they are quite pronounced, such as for an inside curve. Perhaps you are appliquéing the handle on a basket. At the deepest curve on the inside of the handle, clip the seam allowance to within a couple of threads of your marked line at evenly spaced intervals, and be sure to make closer stitches at these points for reinforcement. Using the side and the point of your needle, turn the seam allowance under and make the curve as smooth as possible. If you've created a curve that isn't as smooth as you'd like, use the point of your needle to reshape it before stitching it in place. It might take a few passes before you get it right. Try rolling the needle under the curvature to make it smooth.

POINTS

Creating a perfect point is always a challenge. However, with proper technique and lots of practice, your points *will* improve.

1. Stitch to point you want to fold and turn. Take an extra stitch at this point for reinforcement. (See Fig. 1.) *Note:* Don't sew too close to point before you tuck or you will have very little fabric to work with when making the turn.

Fig. 1

2. Using point of needle, tuck in excess fabric behind shape. (See Fig. 2.)

Fig. 2

3. Move away from point and down next side, working fabric under with point of needle, until edge is smooth. (See Fig. 3.) Use thumb on your opposite hand to press as you go.

Fig. 3

4. Once extra fabric is tucked under and flattened, take an extra stitch at point, make knot through loop in thread to secure point, and pull gently on thread, away from point. (See Fig. 4.)

Fig. 4

5. Stitch down opposite side of shape, using your thumb to press turned edge as you go.

VALLEYS

Valleys have their own unique appliqué process. Examples of valleys ("V") are the cleavage in a heart shape or the dips opposite each point of a star.

1. Stitch to within 1" (2.5 cm) of "V." Make one clip at "V" up to pencil/chalk mark. (See Fig. 5.) *Note:* This is where small, sharp-pointed embroidery scissors come in very handy.

Fig. 5

2. Continue stitching to within 1/4" (.6 cm) of "V."

3. With point of needle, reach over to other side of "V" and turn under seam allowance about 1/4" (.6 cm) to 1/2" (1.3 cm) from "V." (See Fig. 6.)

Fig. 6

4. With point of needle, smooth fabric under, roll needle down through "V" and over to stitched side of "V." Do this two or three times to smooth down entire "V" area. Hold securely with opposite hand and thumb.

5. Stitch down to base of "V." (See Fig. 7.) *Note:* You will see that there is very little, if any, fabric where you clipped. Take three or four stitches to secure this spot. These stitches will show a tiny bit so make them as neat as possible.

Fig. 7

6. Continue stitching up other side of shape.

STEMS AND VINES

There are so many different ways to make stems and vines, but there are two techniques I use most often. One is to make stems and vines with pre-finished edges by using a bias tape maker, and the other is to cut the strips, and then turn and sew one edge by machine and the other by hand. *Note:* If you want to add stems to a meandering vine, sew those on first, before the vine. Position them carefully so that the base of the stem is covered when you sew on the vine.

To make stems and vines with a bias tape maker, simply follow the manufacturer's directions, and then hand appliqué the strips to the quilt. You won't need to turn the edges; the tape maker does this step for you.

The half-machine/half-hand method is simple: Decide on the finished width of the vine or stem, double the finished width, and add ½" (1.3 cm) for seam allowances. So, for example, if you want the strip to finish ¼" (.6 cm) wide, double that measurement to ½" (1.3 cm), add another ½" (1.3 cm) for seam allowances, and cut the strip to measure 1" (2.5 cm). This same basic formula works for strips of any width.

Cut strips that must curve on the bias of the fabric. If the stem or vine requires no curve, you can cut the strips on the straight of grain. In either case, sew strips together end to end with diagonal seams to make a strip of the desired length.

Fold strips in half with wrong sides together and iron using a steam setting. (See Fig. 8.)

Fig. 8

Draw a light guideline on the quilt to indicate where to position the strip. A chalk pencil or #2 lead pencil will work well for this task.

Line up the raw edges of your strip with the vine/stem line and machine sew to quilt using a ¼" (.6 cm) seam allowance. (See Fig. 9.)

Fig. 9

Flip the vine over so that it covers the raw edges and hand appliqué the finished edge. (See Fig. 10.)

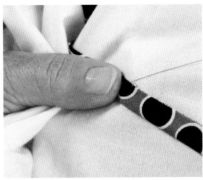

Fig. 10

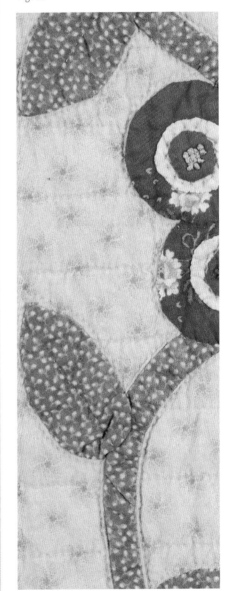

Marking the Quilt

Although the quilt top can be marked for quilting before or after layering, I prefer to mark prior to layering it for basting (see Layering the Quilt).

Use light pressure when using marking tools. If the marks start to wear off before you have quilted them, go back and lightly re-mark them. Do not iron the markings as the heat of the iron could set the marks into the fabric.

Layering the Quilt

Once the quilt top is finished (and marked, if you wish), it is time to layer the top with the backing fabric and the batting. (This is also known as creating the quilt sandwich.) You will need a flat work surface that is large enough to accommodate the entire quilt. At times, I have used my living room floor as my basting surface. Other times I have pushed two or three tables together to make one large work area. I recommend that you use tables if they are available to you—this is much easier on the knees and the back.

To make a quilt sandwich, cut or piece together a backing that is at least 3" (7.6 cm) larger than the quilt top on all sides.

Place the backing right side down on your basting surface and smooth the fabric flat. Using masking tape, tape the center point of each side of the backing to the work surface. Next, tape down each corner of the backing. Gently pull the fabric at each corner to ensure that the backing lays flat. Fill in the area between the centers and the corners with several pieces of tape, always keeping the fabric pulled taut but not stretched. *Note:* If you must work on a carpeted surface, use large straight pins instead of tape to secure the backing in place.

Center the batting on top of the backing and smooth it out, making sure there are no folds or wrinkles. Cut away any batting that extends beyond the backing fabric.

Center and smooth the quilt top right side up on top of the batting.

Using long, straight pins, pin the layers of the quilt together every 8"–10" (20.3–25.4 cm). The pins are merely for stabilization and will be removed as you thread-baste the layers together. Leave the backing taped (or pinned) to the work surface as you complete this process.

Thread a basting needle with a long length of quilting thread and make a large knot at the end. Stitch around the perimeter of the quilt with 2" (5.1 cm)-long stitches, removing the pins as you come to them. When you arrive at your starting point, move in about 3" (7.6 cm) and work around the perimeter of the quilt again. Continue moving in 3" (7.6 cm) at the end of each ring of basting until you reach the center of the quilt. *Note:* When you near the end of the thread, backstitch once, and leave a 6" (15.2 cm) tail instead of creating another knot. Re-thread the needle with another length of thread and continue basting.

After basting is completed, remove the tape. Now you are ready to hand quilt.

Hand Quilting

Hand quilting goes naturally with hand appliqué. I find that both techniques are similar in their meditative qualities. Though I am learning how to machine quilt, hand quilting is closest to my heart.

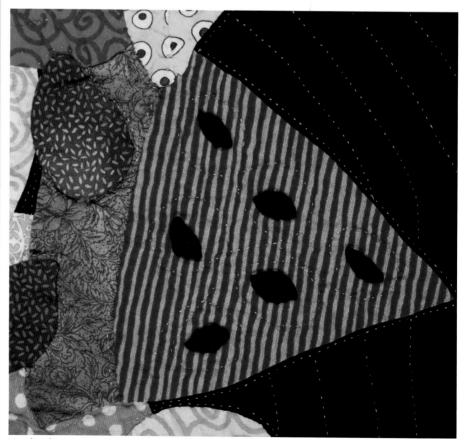

Hand quilting is time consuming, but it is time very well spent.

There are many interesting ways to quilt a quilt. On the border of *Viva Mexico*, I outlined shapes and repeated design elements such as the spiral seen here.

There are a great many books available to teach you the details of hand quilting, and though I will not go into specifics here, I will share a few tips I have learned throughout the years.

Very few items are required for hand quilting. I use #9 or #10 quilting needles; 100-percent glazed cotton quilting thread; a 14" (35.6 cm) round, wooden quilting hoop; and a thimble.

As with all detailed handwork, it is best to have strong, direct light on your work as you hand quilt. Make sure that the light comes from the side that is opposite your stitching hand. This eliminates shadows on the quilt surface.

I like to quilt around my appliqué shapes to give them definition. Some designs need more precise quilting while others can be very loose and freeform. I collect commercially cut stencils and, whenever I can, I use them to create designs for the borders.

If there are a lot of curves in your appliqué design, consider using straight line quilting as a counterpoint. Strive for a balanced amount of quilting over the surface of the quilt—not too much in one area or too little in another.

Hand quilting is a fine-motor skill. As with any such skill, you will get better with practice...and miles and miles of stitches. There really are no short cuts or tricks, but believe me, the effort is worth it. The art of hand quilting is relaxing and fulfilling. The word around our house is, "Don't disturb Mom. She's quilting."

Eye-Catching Quilting Designs

The more hand quilting there is in the background, the more the appliqué designs will pop to the foreground. Repeat design elements whenever possible and hand draw your own shapes and lines at random. Quilting designs are limited only by your imagination; just make sure that your designs enhance the quilt. I recommend that you study as many quilts as you can to learn what type of quilting designs are successful, as well as which designs don't work.

Binding the Quilt

To ensure that your binding is flat and even when it is sewn to the quilt, measure all sides of the quilt carefully, and then carefully measure the binding. When pinning the binding to the quilt, always work from the center out to the corners.

Though there are many ways to bind a quilt, I prefer a double-layer (also called a double-fold) binding.

1. Cut 2½" (6.4 cm) strips of fabric to fit around entire quilt, plus several extra inches for seams and corners. Cut fabric on the straight of grain.

2. Sew the strips of fabric together end to end with diagonal seams to make one long, continuous strip.

3. Fold strip in half with wrong sides together; press. (See Fig. 1.)

Fold

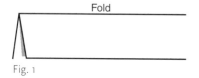

Fig. 1

4. From long pressed strip, cut two strips (length) to the exact measurement of sides of the quilt. Mark center point of each strip and center of the matching side. Use marks to line up raw edges of each strip with raw edge of quilt and sew strip to quilt using a ¼" (.6 cm) seam. (See Fig. 2.) Use a walking foot or even-feed foot to prevent fabric from puckering. Trim batting and backing even with side raw edges of quilt. Flip binding over to back of quilt and sew it down by hand.

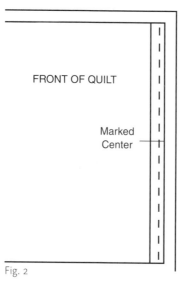

FRONT OF QUILT

Marked Center

Fig. 2

5. From remainder of long pressed strip, cut one strip the width of the quilt top plus 4" (10.2 cm). Mark center of this strip, and mark 2" (5.1 cm) in from each end. Using marks, line up raw edges of strip with raw edge of quilt top and pin. (The 2" (5.1 cm) marks should line up with corners of quilt.) Sew binding to quilt using a ¼" (.6 cm) seam. (See Fig. 3.) Trim batting and backing and flip binding up, but before folding it to back, fold excess fabric in at the corners. Then fold binding over to back of quilt and sew down by hand. *Note:* You may need to trim excess fabric before stitching. Hand stitch corners closed.

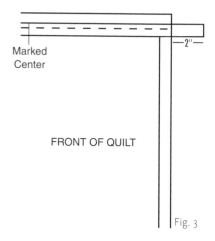

Marked Center

2"

FRONT OF QUILT

Fig. 3

6. Repeat step 5 to cut and stitch binding to bottom edge of quilt.

Bits and Pieces

There are a few additional techniques you will need to complete the projects in this book. I explain them here for easy reference.

FRENCH KNOTS

This easy embroidery knot adds dimension and color to quilts. I used it on *Belinda's Baskets* (page 32).

1. Work two tiny stitches at back of fabric, and then bring thread through to front of fabric.
2. Hold thread taut and wrap it around needle. (See Fig. 4.)
3. Pull thread to gently tighten twists around needle. (See Fig. 5.) While holding thread taut, insert needle into fabric, close to point where it emerged. (See Fig. 6.)
4. Pull needle and thread to back of fabric, leaving loose knot at front. Work two tiny stitches at back to tie off.

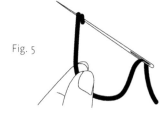

Fig. 4

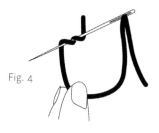

Fig. 5

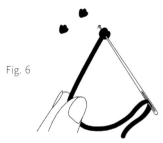

Fig. 6

HALF-SQUARE-TRIANGLE UNITS

There are many ways to make half-square-triangle units. The following method is quick and doesn't require working with a bias edge. This technique produces two half-square-triangle units at a time.

1. Determine finished size of your square unit, and add ⅞" (2.2 cm) to this measurement.
2. Cut two squares from contrasting fabrics and layer them with right sides together.
3. Fold squares in half diagonally and press. (See Fig. 7.) Crease will be used as a sewing guide. (See Fig. 8.)

Fig. 7

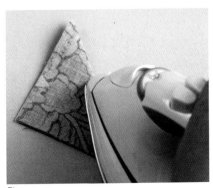

Fig. 8

Press to Impress

To prevent shiny spots, press appliquéd blocks and quilts from the back.

4. Sew a ¼" (.6 cm) seam on each side of center crease. (See Fig. 9.)

Fig. 9

5. Cut along crease line. (See Fig. 10.)

Fig. 10

6. Open and press seam towards darker fabric. Clip extending "ears" off square. (See Fig. 11.)

Fig. 11

You now have two half-square-triangle units that measure the desired finished size plus a ¼" (.6 cm) seam allowance on all sides.

LOG JAMMIN' BLOCK

I use this versatile block often and in many different ways. To construct this log-cabin variation, start with a center square and work around and around the block until you feel like stopping. These blocks are perfect for using up your scraps.

1. Cut a square of any size. This will be center from which block grows.
2. Using a rotary cutter, cut multiple strips of varying widths up to 2" (5.1 cm) wide.
3. Sew a strip of fabric to one side of center square. Cut ends of strip even with center square. (See Fig. 1.)

Fig. 1

4. Working in one direction around center square, continue adding and trimming strips, angling outside edges as desired. (See Fig. 2.) Press all seams towards outside edge of block.

Fig. 2

5. When block is a bit larger than desired, trim and square it to size. (See Fig. 3.)

Fig. 3

As You Like It

When making Log Jammin' blocks, feel free to cut the top of the strips at any angle you desire. Using scissors gives you the freedom to cut irregular angles, which are what make this block so much fun. Don't worry about matching everything up carefully; just cut and sew to your heart's content. Experiment with different strip widths and then decide which look you prefer. Just remember to leave enough fabric for seam allowances.

You may find that a very angular, slanted, funny-shaped block is emerging. Do not worry. You will cut the block to size and square it up at the end. Also, don't be concerned if you lose your spot or change direction when making these blocks. They will still look great and may be even more interesting.

SAWTOOTH BORDER

Here's a popular border that quilt makers have used for generations. It is as versatile now as it was 100 years ago.

1. Cut two squares of same size from contrasting fabrics.
2. Cut each square diagonally to make two triangles (four total).
3. Sew two contrasting triangles together on their long sides. Press units open. (See Fig. 4.)
4. Piece triangle units together, making sure they face the same way. Trim and press. (See Fig. 5.)

Fig. 4

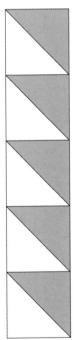

Fig. 5

SPIKY BORDER

This distinctive border is fun and easy to make. As described, the border finishes 4½" (11.4 cm) wide.

1. Cut 6" (15.2 cm)-wide strip each of two contrasting fabrics. Crosscut strips into 2" x 6" (5.1 x 15.2 cm) rectangles. Cut rectangles diagonally from upper left to lower right. (See Fig 1.) **Note:** Rectangles must be cut in same direction. Border will not work if some rectangles are cut in one direction, and others are cut in opposite direction.

2. Sew two contrasting triangles together. (See Fig. 2.)

3. Press unit open. (See Fig. 3.)

4. Piece units together, making sure they face the same way. Trim and press. (See Fig. 4.)

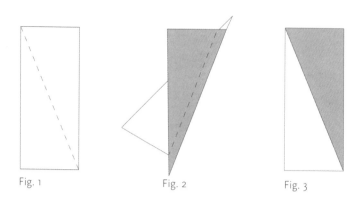

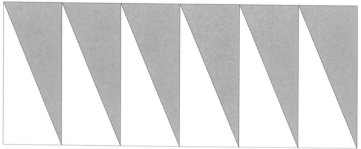

Fig. 1   Fig. 2   Fig. 3

Fig. 4

QUILTER'S KNOT

This knot is perfect for handwork. It is the knot I use most often. Reverse instructions if you are left-handed.

1. Thread needle with single strand of thread.
2. Take end of thread in your left hand and needle in your right hand.
3. Point end of the thread at point of the needle. (See Fig. 5.)
4. Place needle over end of thread, taking hold of thread with your right thumb and index finger. Wrap thread around needle about three times (more if a larger knot is required). (See Fig. 6.)
5. Carefully slide wrapped thread between thumb and index finger of your right hand. Don't let go. (See Fig. 7.)
6. Grasp point of the needle with your left thumb and index finger and, keeping hold of knotted area, pull gently all the way along thread until you feel knot at the end. (See Fig. 8.)

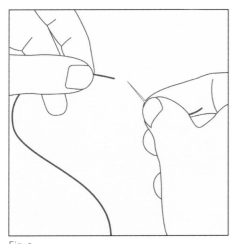

Fig. 5

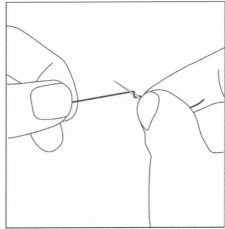

Fig. 6

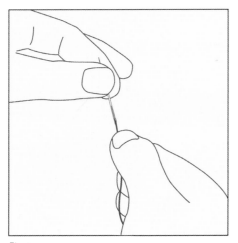

Fig. 7

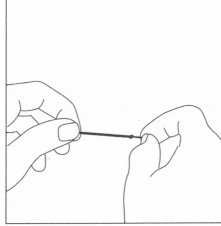

Fig. 8

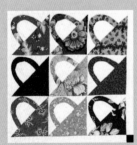

Hand appliqué lends a distinct beauty and quirkiness to my quilts. I am excited to pass on this skill and perhaps help keep this wonderful tradition alive and well.

CHAPTER THREE

FOLK-ART APPLIQUÉD QUILTS

The "container" quilts featured in this chapter tell the story of my appliqué journey. After making *Belinda's Baskets* (page 32), I became more aware of the various kinds of containers that surround me every day. Containers have been a popular element in quilt designs for centuries—I have seen funky-looking pots and vases on hand-appliquéd quilts that were created in the 19th and early 20th centuries. I love studying these antique quilts and always find great ideas to use in my own quilt designs.

After *Belinda's Baskets*, I started designing other kinds of containers, such as those seen in *Golden Goblet* (page 36) and *Window Box* (page 40). Before long, I started thinking of elements (other than flowers) to put in the containers, such as the fruit I featured in *Viva Mexico* (page 50).

To see the changes and progress in my quilts is like reading a diary. The designs in this series of quilts have not changed much through the years, but the colors certainly have. I still like simple shapes and forms, especially circles. It is hard to say whether fabric trends in general are getting brighter, or if I am drawn to bright, vibrant colors more these days. Perhaps it is a combination of the two.

Belinda's Baskets

63" x 63" (160 x 160 cm)
1999

The idea for *Belinda's Baskets* was conceived in 1999. I really was starting to get into appliqué by then, and I had been anxious to do a basket of some sort. As you can see, my mood at the time was soft and romantic. Plus, I had been collecting the luscious Moda fabrics that are so prominent in this quilt.

Belinda's Baskets is a good example of how I work. I had this grand plan for the center block, but no clue as to what might come next. (I love working this way!) Then I discovered a stack of little basket blocks I must have had plans for at one time, and, to my delight, they worked perfectly as a border around the larger medallion basket. If you look closely, you can see that the base of each small basket is a tiny half-square-triangle unit. I had a bunch of these triangles left over and they, too, worked well as one of the borders on the quilt.

I like adding more appliqué whenever I can. The vine-and-leaves border makes a nice frame for the appliqué center in this quilt. I also like to repeat elements from the quilt center whenever I can. A wide border that features the theme fabric pulls everything together.

Fabric

Note: Yardages are based on fabric that measures 42" (106.7 cm) wide.

- Neutral background: 2½ yards (2.29 meters)
- Red center basket: ½ yard (.46 meter)
- Flowers and flower leaves: assorted scraps
- Sawtooth border: assorted print scraps
- Vines and vine leaves: 1 yard (.91 meter)
- Small baskets: assorted scraps of 18 different fabrics **Note:** Each fabric makes 2 baskets.
- Outer border print: 1½ yards (1.37 meters)
- Backing: 4 yards (3.66 meters)
- Binding: ⅔ yard (.60 meter)

Materials

- Appliqué thread in various colors
- Basic quilting supplies
- Cotton batting: approximately 69" x 69" (175.3 x 175.3 cm)
- Embroidery floss in various colors

I love working with circles, so I filled the basket with circle-shaped flowers. Pay attention to your stitches as you work, and remember not to pull your thread too tight.

To Cut Fabric and Prepare for Appliqué

FROM NEUTRAL BACKGROUND FABRIC:

- Cut 1 square, 28½" (72.4 cm), for center appliqué background.✻
- Cut 74 squares, each 1⅞" (4.7 cm), for sawtooth border and Small Basket blocks.
- Cut 4 strips, 6½" (16.5 cm) x width of fabric, for vine background.
- Cut 18 squares, each 3⅞" (9.8 cm), for Small Basket blocks. Cut each square in half diagonally in one direction to yield 2 triangles from each square.
- Cut 72 strips, 3½" x 1½" (8.9 x 3.8 cm), for Small Basket blocks.
- Cut 9 squares, each 6¼" (15.8 cm), for side triangles. Cut each square diagonally in both directions to yield 4 triangles from each square.
- Cut 2 squares, each 3½" (8.9 cm), for corner triangles. Cut each square in half diagonally in one direction to yield 2 triangles from each square.

✻ You will trim this block to measure 27½" x 27½" (69.9 x 69.9 cm) when appliqué is complete and before adding borders.

FROM RED CENTER BASKET FABRIC:

- Cut 1 square, 12" (30.5 cm). Cut in half diagonally in one direction to yield 2 triangles. One half-square triangle is for basket body. From remaining half-square triangle, cut one basket base using Large Basket Base template (page 92).
- Cut one basket handle using Large Basket Handle template (page 93).

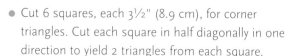

FROM FLOWER AND FLOWER LEAF SCRAPS:
- Cut assorted flower and flower leaf shapes using templates A-Z and AA-FF (pages 92–93).
- Cut 16 flower shapes using Vine Flower template (page 93).

FROM SAWTOOTH BORDER FABRIC:
- Cut 56 squares, each 1⅞" (4.7 cm), for sawtooth border.

FROM VINE AND VINE LEAF FABRIC:
- Cut enough 1" (2.5 cm)-wide bias strips to equal approximately 160" (406.4 cm) when sewn together end to end.
- Cut 75 vine leaves using Vine Leaf template (page 93).

FROM SMALL BASKET BLOCK FABRIC:
- Cut 18 squares, each 3⅞" (9.8 cm), for Small Basket blocks. Cut each square in half diagonally in one direction to yield 2 triangles from each square.
- Cut 36 small basket handles—2 to match each 3⅞" square above—using Small Basket Handle template (page 93).
- Cut 18 squares, each 1⅞" (4.7 cm), for Small Basket blocks and sawtooth border.

FROM OUTER-BORDER FABRIC:
- Cut 9 squares, each 6¼" (15.8 cm), for side triangles. Cut each square diagonally in both directions to yield 4 triangles from each square.

- Cut 6 squares, each 3½" (8.9 cm), for corner triangles. Cut each square in half diagonally in one direction to yield 2 triangles from each square.
- Cut six strips, 5½" (14 cm) x width of fabric.

FROM BINDING FABRIC:
- Cut 7 strips, 2½" (6.4 cm) x width of fabric.

To Assemble Quilt Top

Note: Use ¼" (.6 cm)-wide seam allowances for all piecing. Press seams as you go. Refer to quilt photo (page 32), How to Appliqué (page 17), and Additional Appliqué Techniques (page 19) as needed.

1. Appliqué large basket (body and base) and large basket handle to 28½" (72.4 cm) neutral background square.
2. Layer flower and flower leaf shapes on background. Take photograph of design.
3. Remove top layers of shapes until only bottom layer of appliqué shapes remain. Pin shapes to background and appliqué in place.
4. Repeat until all shapes have been appliquéd to center basket. Embroider center of flowers with French knots (page 25).
5. Working approximately 2" (5.1 cm) from corners, appliqué flowers and leaves in corners of background square. Embroider center of flowers with French knots.
6. Trim center block to 27½" (69.9 cm) square.

I repeated the circles on the swags as a way to tie all the quilt elements together. French knots in the center of the flowers add interest and whimsy.

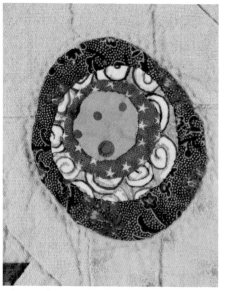

When appliquéing the flowers to the quilt, feel free to layer them in unexpected ways. This is folk art, after all—let your personality show through.

The double-layer binding will hold up well over time. I quilted soft lines along the border because the fabric is so busy.

The points of the sawtooth border echo the points on the baskets and provide a pretty frame for the center of the quilt.

Crosshatch quilting works well with the lines of the center basket.

7. Refer to Half-Square-Triangle Units (page 25) and Sawtooth Border (page 27). Using 1⅞ (4.7 cm) neutral squares and 1⅞" (4.7 cm) Small Basket and assorted print squares, make 148 half-square-triangle units. Set 36 Small Basket units aside. Sew together 27 remaining half-square-triangle units. Make 2 strips, and then sew one strip to each side of quilt. Sew together 29 remaining half-square-triangle units. Make 2 strips, and sew one strip to top of quilt and one strip to bottom.

8. Sew four 6½" (16.5 cm)-wide neutral background strips together end to end to make one long strip. From this strip, cut two 29½" (75 cm)-long side strips and two 41½" (105.4 cm)-long top and bottom strips. Sew side strips to quilt first, and then sew top and bottom strips to quilt.

9. Appliqué small basket handles to neutral half-square triangles. Sew appliquéd handle triangle to matching basket body triangle to form a square. Sew one 3½" x 1½" (8.9 x 3.8 cm) neutral rectangle to side of basket square. Sew one 3½" x 1½" (8.9 x 3.8 cm) rectangle to matching half-square-triangle unit set aside in step 7. Sew this unit to the basket/rectangle unit to complete block. Make 36 Small Basket blocks.

10. Arrange and sew neutral and print side triangles to each of the eight Small Basket blocks. Sew units together. Make 2 for sides of quilt.

11. Sew one neutral corner triangle and one print corner triangle to each corner, being careful to place them on correct corners—neutral fabric triangle on inside corner and print triangle on outside corner. Trim excess triangle fabric, being careful to leave ¼" (.6 cm) seam allowance on all sides. *Note:* If basket strips come out a bit long, trim them to fit.

12. Arrange and sew triangles and Small Basket blocks to make top and bottom Small Basket borders; trim as needed. *Note:* All corner triangles are now print border fabric.

13. Sew 5½" (14 cm)-wide print outer-border strips together end to end to make one long strip. From this strip, cut two 52½" (133.4 cm)-long side border strips and two 62½" (158.8 cm)-long top and bottom border strips.

14. Sew side strips to quilt first, and then sew top and bottom strips to quilt.

To Finish Quilt

To finish quilt, refer to Techniques on pages 16–29, or finish using desired methods.

Since this is such an old fashioned-looking quilt I hand quilted the top using a classic double-line crosshatch on the center block. You will find this technique used quite often on antique quilts. I also used lots of outline quilting to accentuate the vines, leaves, and flowers. The outer border print fabric is very busy, so it was difficult to mark for quilting. To overcome this challenge, I quilted some soft, meandering lines on the border and to offset the large amount of straight-line quilting on the center of the quilt.

Golden Goblet

56" x 65" (142.2 x 165.1 cm)
2000

I made *Golden Goblet* immediately following *Belinda's Baskets* (page 32). After working with all the small appliqué pieces and details in *Belinda's Baskets*, I was ready to go big...and I have always loved circles.

The fabric I used for the goblet is a bit unusual, and I felt compelled to include it in this quilt. The swags are my homage to an element often found in antique quilts. Repeating the circles with the swags ties all the elements in the quilt together.

Working one layer at a time is the only way to appliqué these shapes. Make sure to match thread to each appliqué as you sew.

Fabric

Note: Yardages are based on fabric that measures 42" (106.7 cm) wide.

- Neutral border background: 2 yards (1.83 meters)
- Red inner border and swags: 2 yards (1.83 meters)
- Neutral center-block background: 1 yard (.91 meter)
- Green sawtooth border: ½ yard (.46 meter)
- Golden goblet: 1 fat quarter
- Purple swag flowers: ¼ yard (.23 meter) or 1 fat quarter
- Large, medium, and small circle flowers and flower centers: assorted scraps
- Small green circles (for purple flower centers): assorted scraps
- Backing: 3½ yards (3.20 meters)
- Binding: ⅔ yard (.60 meter)

Materials

- Appliqué thread in various colors
- Basic quilting supplies
- Cotton batting: approximately 62" x 71" (157.5 x 180.3 cm)

To Cut Fabric and Prepare for Appliqué

NEUTRAL CENTER-BLOCK BACKGROUND FABRIC:

- Cut 1 piece, 30½" x 39½" (77.5 x 100.4 cm).

FROM GOLDEN GOBLET FABRIC:

- Cut one goblet using Golden Goblet template (page 94).

LARGE, MEDIUM, AND SMALL CIRCLE FLOWER AND FLOWER CENTER SCRAPS:

- Cut 10 large circle flowers using Large Circle Flower and Large Circle Flower Center templates (page 96).
- Cut 10 medium circle flowers using Medium Circle Flower and Medium Circle Flower Center templates (page 95).
- Cut 10 small circle flowers using Small Circle Flower and Small Circle Flower Center templates (page 95).

FROM RED INNER-BORDER AND SWAG FABRIC:

- Cut two strips, 2" x 39½" (5.1 x 100.4 cm), for side inner borders.
- Cut two strips, 2" x 33½" (5.1 x 85.1 cm), for top and bottom inner borders.
- Cut 14 border swag shapes using Swag Border template (page 96).
- Cut 4 corner swag shapes using Corner Swag template (page 97).

FROM GREEN SAWTOOTH BORDER FABRIC:

- Cut 25 squares, each 3⅞" (9.8 cm).

The red inner border provides the perfect resting place for the next border of half-square-triangle units.

FROM OUTER-BORDER NEUTRAL FABRIC:
- Cut 25 squares, each 3⅞" (9.8 cm), for sawtooth border.
- Cut 4 squares, each 3½" (8.9 cm), for sawtooth border.
- Cut 4 strips, 8½" (21.6 cm) x width of fabric, for outer border.

FROM PURPLE SWAG FLOWER FABRIC:
- Cut 18 purple swag flowers using Purple Flower template (page 95).

FROM ASSORTED SMALL GREEN SCRAPS:
- Cut 18 small circle shapes using Purple Flower Center template (page 95).

FROM BINDING FABRIC:
- Cut 6 strips, 2½" (6.4 cm) x width of fabric.

To Assemble Quilt Top

Note: Use ¼" (.6 cm)-wide seam allowances for all piecing. Press seams as you go. Refer to quilt photo (page 36), How to Appliqué (page 17), and Additional Appliqué Techniques (page 19) as needed.

1. Appliqué goblet shape to center of 30½" x 39½" (77.5 x 100.4 cm) neutral background piece.

2. Layer large, medium, and small circle flower and flower center shapes on background. Take photograph of design.

3. Remove top layers of shapes until only bottom layer of appliqué shapes remain. Pin shapes to background and appliqué in place.

4. Repeat until all shapes have been appliquéd to center block.

5. Sew 2" x 39½" (5.1 x 100.4 cm) red inner borders to sides of quilt, and then 2" x 33½" (5.1 x 85.1 cm) red inner borders to top and bottom of quilt.

6. Refer to Half-Square-Triangle Units (page 25) and Sawtooth Border (page 27). Using 3⅞" (9.8 cm) neutral squares and 3⅞" (9.8 cm) green squares, make 50 half-square-triangle units for sawtooth border. Sew together 14 half-square-triangle units. Make 2 strips and then sew one strip to each side of quilt. Sew together 11 half-square-triangle units, placing a 3½" (8.9 cm) neutral square at each end. Make 2 strips, and then sew one strip to top of quilt and one strip to bottom of quilt.

7. Sew 8 ½" (1.3 cm)-wide neutral outer-border strips together end to end to make one long strip. From this strip, cut two 48½" (123.2 cm)-long side border strips and two 55½" (141 cm)-long top/bottom border strips. Sew side strips to quilt first, and then sew top and bottom strips to quilt.

8. Position 4 border swags evenly on each side outer border and 3 border swags evenly on top and bottom outer borders. Place corner swags in corners. They may overlap a little bit, but should fit just fine once they've been appliquéd. (It's no problem if they don't fit exactly; the purple flowers will cover any slight variations.) Lightly mark placement of swags, and then remove swags.

9. Working one side at a time, appliqué swags.

10. Appliqué purple flower and green flower center shapes in place on swag.

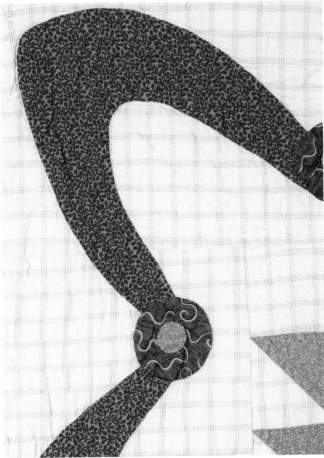

The purple flowers cover the ends of the swags and repeat the flower shapes in the goblet.

Each portion of the background is quilted with different designs. I love how the squares look like little pillows.

To Finish Quilt

To finish quilt, refer to Techniques on pages 16–29, or finish using desired methods.

The hand quilting on this piece is very simple. Wherever there are lots of soft edges, circles, and curves (such as goblet and round flowers), use straight line quilting in the background to set off the shapes. A classic diagonal cross-hatch works well on the center block of *Golden Goblet*. Notice the straight lines of hand quilting behind the swag border.

Straight-line quilting works well on busy fabric and to complement curved shapes.

Window Box

69" x 58" (175.3 x 147.3 cm)
2001

Our small cottage in the little mountain community of Camp Sherman, Oregon, has wonderful old windows and doors that we have collected from junkyards and antique shops over the years, and we have placed window boxes under several of the windows. We have a lot of shade in our yard because of the big Ponderosa Pine trees, but I just stuff the boxes full of shade-loving plants and cross my fingers that we might get a little bit of color.

Window Box is what I *wish* my window boxes looked like. As always, I have used simple shapes and whimsical accents. Once I positioned the flowers, it became obvious that I needed more going on toward the top of the quilt, so I added the vine.

When you are doing appliqué, be sure to stay open-minded to changes along the way. The quilt will tell you what it needs.

Fabric

Note: Yardages are based on fabrics that measure 42" (106.7 cm) wide.

- Siding/background: 1¾ yards (1.60 meters)
- Shutters: 1 yard (.91 meter)
- Windowpanes: ⅔ yard (.60 meter)
- Window sashing and trim: ½ yard (.46 meter)
- Window box: ½ yard (.46 meter)
- Vines: ½ yard (.46 meter)
- Trees on shutters: 1 fat quarter
- Flowers: scraps of at least 25 different colors and prints
- Leaves: assorted scraps approximately ⅔ yard (.60 cm) total
- Backing: 4 yards (3.66 meters)
- Binding: ⅔ yard (.60 meter)

Materials

- Appliqué thread in various colors
- Basic quilting supplies
- Cotton batting: approximately 75" x 64" (190.5 x 162.6 cm)

I used sashing strips here to create the window frame. The flowers and vines were added after the window was "built."

To Cut Fabric and Prepare for Appliqué

FROM WINDOWPANE FABRIC:

- Cut 9 rectangles, 8" x 10" (20.3 x 25.4 cm).

FROM WINDOW SASHING AND TRIM FABRIC:

- Cut 3 strips, 1½" (3.8 cm) x width of fabric. From these strips, cut 2 strips, 25" (63.5 cm) long and 6 strips, 10" (25.4 cm) long.
- Cut 3 strips, 2½" (6.4 cm) x width of fabric. From these strips, cut 2 strips, 31" (78.7 cm) long, for sides of window, and 1 strip, 29" (73.7 cm) long, for top of window.

I used a couple of different fabrics for the leaves. For a realistic-looking vine, cut some leaves in reverse and fan them out in different directions.

The starkness of the tree fabric makes the shape really "pop" from the quilt.

FROM SHUTTER FABRIC:

- Cut 2 rectangles, 15" x 33" (38.1 x 83.8 cm).

FROM TREE FABRIC (SHUTTERS):

- Cut 2 trees using Tree template (page 99).

FROM SIDING FABRIC:

- Cut 2 strips, 6" (15.2 cm) x width of fabric, for siding above window.
- Cut 2 strips, 6" x 33" (15.2 x 83.8 cm), for siding next to shutters.
- Cut 2 strips, 12½" x 20½" (31.8 x 52.1 cm), for siding next to window box.
- Cut 2 strips, 8" (20.3 cm) x width of fabric, for siding below window box.

FROM WINDOW BOX FABRIC:

- Cut 1 rectangle, 29" x 12½" (73.7 x 31.8 cm).

FROM VINE FABRIC:

- Cut enough 1" (2.5 cm)-wide bias strips (for use with ½" (1.3 cm) bias tape maker) to equal approximately 140" (355.6 cm) when sewn together end to end.

FROM LEAF FABRICS:

- Cut 90 leaves using Leaf template (page 99).

FROM FLOWER FABRICS:

- Cut assorted flower shapes using templates A-P (pages 98–99).

FROM BINDING FABRIC:

- Cut 7 strips, 2½" (6.4 cm) x width of fabric.

To Assemble Quilt Top

Note: Use ¼" (.6 cm)-wide seam allowances for all piecing. Press seams as you go. Refer to quilt photo (page 40), How to Appliqué (page 17), and Additional Appliqué Techniques (page 19) as needed.

1. Sew three 8" x 10" (20.3 x 25.4 cm) windowpane rectangles and two 1½" x 10" (3.8 x 25.4 cm) window sashing strips together, alternating them to make a horizontal row. Make 3 window sections. Sew sections together, alternating them with two 1½" x 25" (3.8 x 63.5 cm) horizontal sashing strips. *Note:* Carefully mark horizontal sashing strips to indicate where vertical sashing meets horizontal sashing; this helps keep windowpanes aligned.

2. Sew on 2½" x 31" (6.4 x 78.7 cm) side window trim strips.

3. Sew on 2½" x 29" (6.4 x 73.7 cm) top window trim strip.

4. Appliqué 1 tree shape to each 15" x 33" (38.1 x 83.8 cm) shutter.

5. Sew 1 appliquéd shutter to each side of window unit.

6. Sew 6" x 33" (15.2 x 83.8 cm) siding strips to side of shutters.

7. Sew 2 siding strips, 6" (15.2 cm) x width of fabric together end to end. From this strip, cut 1 strip 69" (175.3 cm) long and sew to top of quilt.

8. Sew 12½" x 20½" (31.8 x 52.1 cm) siding rectangles to each side of 29" x 12½" (73.7 x 31.8 cm) window box.

9. Sew unit from step 8 to bottom of unit from step 7, being careful to line up box with window. *Note:* The bottom siding strip can be added as the final step. There is a lot of fabric to deal with as you appliqué this quilt, and anytime you can have less fabric to manage, the better.

10. Layer flower shapes and vine and leaf shapes on background. Take photograph of design.

11. Remove top layers of shapes until only bottom layer of appliqué shapes remain. Pin shapes to background and appliqué in place.

12. Repeat until all shapes have been appliquéd to quilt.

13. When all appliqué is completed, sew two, 8" (20.3 cm)-wide siding strips together end to end. From this strip, cut one 69" (175.3 cm) strip and sew to bottom of quilt.

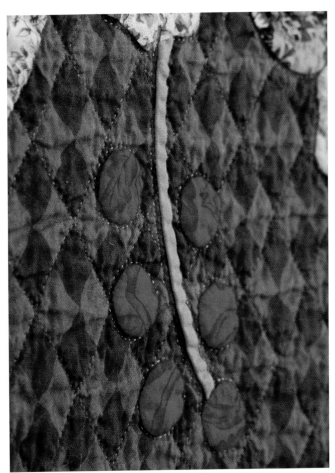

When it comes to bias stems, make more than you think you will need. That way, you will have enough on hand to add unexpected touches.

The flowers growing in this window box fill my home with color, even during the most dreary winter months.

To Finish Quilt

To finish quilt, refer to Techniques on pages 16–29, or finish using desired methods.

The hand quilting on this piece is very simple. Think of some of the quaint cottages you have seen, and the decorative details that make them so charming. Incorporate those details into your hand quilting.

On the siding, I used an overall scallop pattern that is reminiscent of detailed shingles. Notice that I quilted a simple pattern on the shutters that hints of wooden slats.

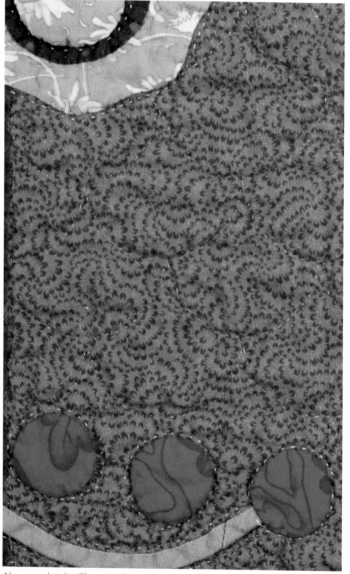

Above and right: The wavy lines of quilting give movement to the plain background fabrics.

Heirloom Roses

62" x 62" (157.5 x 157.5 cm)
2002

The design for *Heirloom Roses* springs from the border fabric. I loved this print fabric so much that I purchased a few yards as soon as I saw it. Shortly thereafter, I discovered some leftover pieces of sateen fabric from another quilt that went perfectly with the print fabric. Once I put the fabrics together, I felt they called for a more elegant, formal design.

The colors in the fabrics remind me of old-fashioned roses. The sateen is heaven to hand quilt, so I made sure there were lots of open spaces where the quilting would show. Notice how I used the Heirloom Rose template to mark the quilting design in the large, open triangles.

Fabrics

Note: Yardages are based on fabrics that measure 42" (106.7 cm) wide.

- Brown background: 2 ½ yards (2.29 meters)
- Black sashing and vase: ⅔ yard (.60 meter)
- Outer-border and sawtooth-border print: 1⅓ yard (1.21 meters)
- Roses: ¼ yard (.23 meter) or 1 fat quarter each of 5 different colors
- Backing: 4 yards (3.66 meters)
- Binding: ⅔ yard (.60 meter)

Materials

- Appliqué thread in various colors
- Basic quilting supplies
- Cotton batting: approximately 68" x 68" (172.7 x 172.7 cm)
- Plastic template sheet

To Cut Fabric and Prepare for Appliqué

FROM BROWN BACKGROUND FABRIC:

- Cut 1 square, 30½" (77.5 cm), for center square.
- Cut 2 squares, each 26½" (67.3 cm), for large corner triangles. Cut each square in half diagonally in one direction to yield 2 triangles from each square.
- Cut 34 squares, each 2⅞" (7.3 cm), for sawtooth border.

FROM EACH ROSE FABRIC:

- Cut 6 roses (30 total) using Heirloom Rose template (page 100). *Note:* Template will be used to cut multiple spirals, so cut template from a plastic template sheet.

Cut the spiral template from template plastic since the shape will be used many times.

FROM BLACK FABRIC:

- Cut 1 vase, using Vase template (page 100).
- Cut 2 strips, 1½" x 30½" (3.8 x 77.5 cm), and 2 strips, 1½" x 32½" (3.8 x 82.5 cm), for inner sashing.
- Cut 5 strips, 1½" (3.8 cm) x width of fabric, for inner border.

FROM OUTER-BORDER AND SAWTOOTH-BORDER PRINT FABRIC:

- Cut 34 squares, each 2⅞" (7.3 cm), for sawtooth border.
- Cut 6 strips, 5" (12.7 cm) x width of fabric, for outer border.

FROM BINDING FABRIC:

- Cut 7 strips, 2½" (6.4 cm) x width of fabric.

To Assemble Quilt Top

Note: Use ¼" (.6 cm)-wide seam allowances for all piecing. Press seams as you go. Refer to quilt photo (page 45), How to Appliqué (page 17), and Additional Appliqué Techniques (page 19) as needed.

1. Appliqué vase on-point in 30½" (77.5 cm) brown center square.

2. Beginning on bottom row, position one rose at a time and appliqué to background. Be sure to overlap each rose a little bit.

3. Sew one 1½" x 30½" (3.8 x 77.5 cm) black inner-sashing strip to opposite sides of center square, and then 1½" x 32½" (3.8 x 82.5 cm) black inner-sashing strips to remaining sides.

4. Refer to Half-Square-Triangle Units (page 25) and Sawtooth Border (page 27). Using 2⅞" (7.3 cm) brown squares and 2⅞" (7.3 cm) print squares, make 68 half-square-triangle units for sawtooth border. Sew together 16 half-square-triangle units. Make 2 strips, and then sew 1 strip to opposite sides of center square. Sew together 18 half-square-triangle units. Make 2 strips, and then sew them to remaining sides of center square.

5. Center and sew 2 large brown corner triangles to opposite sides of quilt. Sew 2 large brown corner triangles to remaining sides.

6. Trim and square quilt to 51½" (130.8 cm) square.

Black sashing and binding really set off the print border on *Heirloom Roses.*

7. Sew 1½" (3.8 cm) black strips together end to end to make one long strip. From this strip, cut two 51½" (130.8 cm)-long side inner-border strips and two 53½" (135.9 cm)-long top and bottom inner-border strips. Sew side strips to quilt first, and then sew top and bottom strips to quilt.

8. Sew 5" (12.7 cm) print outer-border strips together end to end to make one long strip. From this strip, cut two 53½" (135.9 cm)-long side outer-border strips and two 62½" (158.8 cm)-long top and bottom outer-border strips. Sew side strips to quilt first, and then sew top and bottom strips to quilt.

To Finish Quilt

To finish quilt, refer to Techniques on pages 16–29, or finish using desired methods.

The dense quilting in the center block was achieved with a crosshatch design. Notice quilting in the large center triangles; I used the Heirloom Rose template to draw these shapes. Because the outer border print fabric is very busy, I used straight-line quilting.

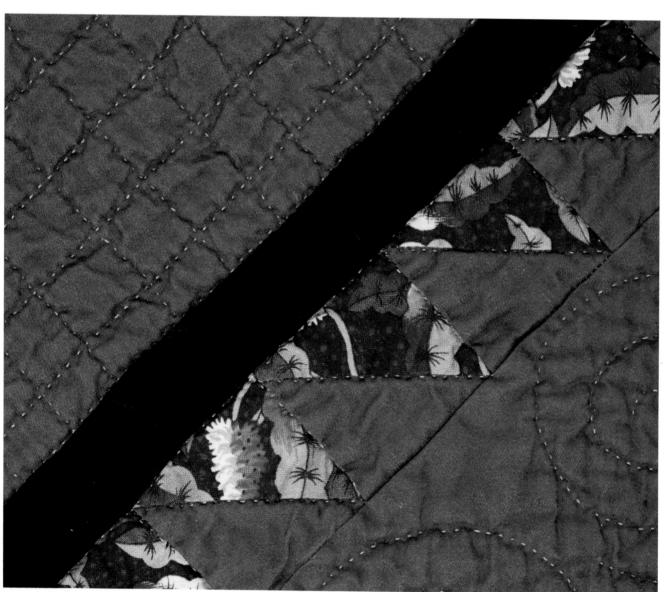

Using the background fabric in the half-square-triangle border makes the contrasting colorful print fabric really stand out.

Contrasting thread brings out the quilting design on the vase.

Viva Mexico

65" x 66" (165.1 x 167.6 cm)
2004

*V*iva Mexico carries some very fond memories for me. In the fall of 2002, my husband, Doug, and our boys, Ande and Charlie, who were then 12 and 14 years old, set sail out of Portland, Oregon, for a nine-month voyage to Mexico. This quilt was my appliqué project for the trip. I have always loved the big, brightly painted platters and bowls that can be found in Mexico. The shapes and colors used in the fruit and vegetable appliqués are reminiscent of classic Mexican folk art.

Fabrics

Note: Yardages are based on fabrics that measure 42" (106.7 cm) wide. In this quilt, the vine is a narrow pieced sashing strip rather than an appliquéd element.

- Black center-block background: 1¼ yards (1.14 meters)
- Outer-border print: 1¼ yards (1.14 meters)
- Black leaf background border: 1 yard (.91 meter)
- Basket and "vine" sashing: 1 yard (.91 meter)
- Leaves: 1 yard (.91 meter)
- Red-striped inner border/sash: ⅓ yard (.30 meter)
- Fruit: assorted scraps or fat quarters
- Spirals: assorted scraps
- Backing: 4 yards (3.66 meters)
- Binding: ⅔ yard (.60 cm) total of assorted fabrics

Materials

- Appliqué thread in various colors
- Basic quilting supplies
- Cotton batting: approximately 71" x 72" (180.3 x 182.90 cm)
- Plastic template sheet

To Cut Fabric and Prepare for Appliqué

FROM BLACK CENTER-BLOCK BACKGROUND FABRIC:

- Cut 1 piece, 38½" x 39½" (97.8 x 100.4 cm).＊

FROM BASKET AND "VINE" SASHING FABRIC:

- Cut 1 basket using Basket Base template (page 101).
- Cut 1 basket handle using Basket Handle template (page 101).
- Cut 5 strips, 1" (2.5 cm) x width of fabric, for "vine" sashing.

＊ You will trim this block to measure 37½" x 38½" (95.3 x 97.8 cm) when appliqué is complete and before adding borders.

Though the handle was thread-basted, I clipped the basting where necessary to add the underlying shapes.

FROM FRUIT FABRICS:

- Cut assorted fruit shapes using Large Plum, Pear, Pear Top, Small Plum, Lemon, Apple Leaf, Large Apple, Small Apple, Grape Stem A, Grape Stem B, Large Grape, Small Grape, Orange, Large Banana, Small Banana, Melon, Seed, Melon Rind, Pineapple Top, and Pineapple Base templates (pages 101–107).

FROM RED-STRIPED BORDER/SASH FABRIC:

- Cut 4 strips, 2" (5.1 cm) x width of fabric.

FROM BLACK LEAF BACKGROUND FABRIC:

- Cut 11 strips, 3½" (8.9 cm) x width of fabric.

FROM LEAF FABRIC:

- Cut 148 leaves using Border Leaf template (page 103).

FROM SPIRAL FABRICS:

- Cut 16 spirals using Spiral template (page 106). *Note:* Template will be used to cut multiple spirals, so cut template from a template plastic sheet.

FROM OUTER-BORDER PRINT:

- Cut 6 strips, 6½" (16.5 cm) x width of fabric.

FROM BINDING FABRIC:

- Cut 7 strips, 2½" (6.4 cm) x width of fabric.

To Assemble Quilt Top

Note: Use ¼" (.6 cm)-wide seam allowances for all piecing. Press seams as you go. Refer to quilt photo (page 50), How to Appliqué (page 17), and Additional Appliqué Techniques (page 19) as needed.

1. Center basket and handle on 38½" x 39½" (97.8 x 100.4 cm) black background piece. Thread-baste basket to background, leaving top edge open to insert handle and fruit. Arrange fruit in basket as desired. *Note:* This is a whimsical design, so do not spend "a bunch" of time fussing with a realistic arrangement.

2. Thread-baste handle. *Note:* Some basting stitches will be cut later to position pineapple under handle. Take photograph of appliqué design.

I used a variety of fabrics for the binding and I love the whimsical look.

Grapes add dimension and weight to the basket.

To tie all the elements together, I added spirals in colors found throughout the quilt.

3. Remove top layers of shapes until only bottom layer of appliqué shapes remain. Pin shapes to background and appliqué in place.

4. Repeat until all shapes have been appliquéd to center block. Finish appliquéing top of basket.

5. Trim center block to 37½" x 38½" (95.3 x 97.8 cm).

6. Sew 2" (5.1 cm)-wide red striped border/sash strips together end to end to make one long strip. From this strip, cut two 38½" (97.8)-long side strips, and two 40½" (102.9 cm)-long top and bottom strips. Sew side strips to quilt first, then sew top and bottom strips to quilt.

7. Sew 3½" (8.9 cm)-wide black leaf background strips together end to end to make one long strip. From this long strip, cut two 41½" (105.4 cm)-long side inner-background strips and two 46½" (118.1 cm)-long top and bottom inner-background strips. Sew side strips to quilt first, and then sew top and bottom strips to quilt.

8. Sew 1" (2.5 cm)-wide "vine" sashing strips together end to end to make one long strip. From this long strip, cut four 47½" (120.7 cm)-long side, top, and bottom "vine" strips. Sew side strips to quilt first, and then sew top and bottom strips to quilt.

9. From remaining long strip from step 7, cut two 48½" (123.2 cm)-long side outer-background strips, and two 53½" (135.9 cm)-long top and bottom outer-background strips. Sew side strips to quilt first, and then sew top and bottom strips to quilt.

10. Working one side at a time, position 18 border leaf shapes on each vine background, with leaves radiating from each side of "vine" sashing. Place spiral shape at midpoint, where leaves change direction. Appliqué leaves and spirals in place.

11. Appliqué three spiral shapes and one border leaf shape in each corner.

12. Sew 6½" (16.5 cm) outer-border strips together end to end to make one long strip. From this strip, cut two 54½" (138.4 cm) side outer-border strips, and two 65½" (166.4 cm) top and bottom outer-border strips. Sew side strips to quilt first, and then sew top and bottom strips to quilt.

To Finish Quilt

To finish quilt, refer to Techniques on pages 16–29, or finish using desired methods.

The center of this quilt was quilted with an echo effect. It would also look great with a crosshatch design in the background. Instead, I just eyeballed the echo lines and went on my merry way. Rather than quilting around each leaf separately, I meandered around each leaf with a continuous wavy line. Since the outer border is such a busy print, I drew and quilted big, loose spirals as I went along.

Limeade

37" x 37" (94 x 94 cm)
2005

Black is a dramatic and eye-catching color. I enjoy incorporating it into my quilts, and found it worked especially well as a backdrop for these bright and colorful flowers.

Limeade was inspired by a workshop led by well-known Michigan quilter Gwen Marston. I have long admired Gwen's style and she has had a big influence on how I approach quilt design—pretty much anything goes. If it pleases you, go for it. I like knowing that I am not beholden to too many rules. It is so freeing to realize that I can do just about anything I want...and you can, too.

Limeade is based on a traditional pattern, but it has been jazzed up with vibrant color and whimsical shapes. The exaggerated border certainly makes a bold statement. Always consider mixing things up. Do the unexpected. The borders don't always need to match. Make your mark and don't look back.

Fabrics

Note: Yardages are based on fabric that measures 42" (106.7 cm) wide.

- Black background: 1½ yards (1.37 meters)
- Spiky border: ½ yard (.46 meter) lime green and ¼ yard (.23 meter) red
- Stems: ½ yard (.46 meter)
- Vase: 1 fat quarter or scrap measuring approximately 10" x 12" (25.4 x 30.5 cm)
- Flowers, leaves, and star: multiple colorful scraps
- Backing: 1¼ yards (1.14 meters)
- Binding: ½ yard (.46 meter)

Materials

- Appliqué thread in various colors
- Basic quilting supplies
- Cotton batting: approximately 43" x 43" (109.2 x 109.2 cm)

To Cut Fabric and Prepare for Appliqué

Note: All rectangles for spiky border *must* be cut in the same direction. Refer to Spiky Border (page 28) as needed.

FROM BLACK BACKGROUND FABRIC:

- Cut 1 square, 29½" (75 cm) for center square.✻
- Cut 2 strips, 6" (15.2 cm) x width of fabric. Cut strips into 36 rectangles, 2" x 6" (5.1 x 15.2 cm). Cut rectangles diagonally from upper left to lower right.

FROM VASE FABRIC:

- Cut 1 vase using Vase template (page 108).

FROM STEM FABRICS:

- Cut assorted bias strips to make stems using ¼" (.6 mm) or ½" (1.3 cm) bias tape maker.

FROM FLOWER, LEAF, AND STAR FABRICS:

- Cut various flower and leaf shapes using templates A–K (pages 108–111).
- Cut 1 star using Star template (page 109).
- Cut 1 star circle using Star Circle template (page 109).

✻ You will trim this block to measure 28½" x 28½" (72.4 x 72.4 cm) when appliqué is complete and before adding borders.

Outline quilting lets the star appliqué shine brightly.

FROM RED SPIKY-BORDER FABRIC:

- Cut 1 strip, 6" (15.2 cm) x width of fabric. Cut strip into 10 rectangles, 2" x 6" (5.1 x 15.2 cm). Cut rectangles diagonally from upper left to lower right.

FROM LIME GREEN SPIKY-BORDER FABRIC:

- Cut 2 strips, 6" (15.2 cm) x width of fabric. Cut strips into 26 rectangles, 2" x 6" (5.1 x 15.2 cm). Cut rectangles diagonally from upper left to lower right.

FROM BINDING FABRIC:

- Cut 4 strips, 2½" (6.4 cm) x width of fabric.

Let your imagination run wild when choosing fabrics for the flowers and vines.

To Assemble Quilt Top

Note: Use ¼" (.6 cm)-wide seam allowances for all piecing. Press seams as you go. Refer to quilt photo (page 54), How to Appliqué (page 17), and Additional Appliqué Techniques (page 19) as needed.

1. Appliqué vase to 29½" (75 cm) black background square, leaving top of vase open for insertion of stems. *Note:* You can also appliqué the vase after all stems have been appliquéd.

2. Insert stems well inside top of vase. Appliqué stems in place. Appliqué top of vase closed. Appliqué star and star circle shapes on top of vase.

3. Position and pin flower and leaf shapes to background, and then appliqué in place.

4. Trim background to 28½" (72.4 cm) square.

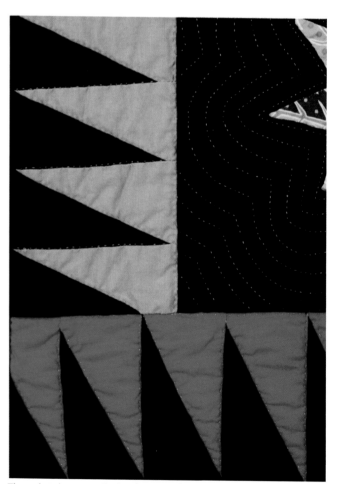

The red and green spiky borders provide a simple but stunning frame for the container.

5. Refer to Spiky Border (page 28) and use black rectangles and red rectangles to make 20 red units, and black rectangles and lime green rectangles to make 52 green units. Sew together 16 lime green-and-black units. Make 2 strips, and then sew them to sides of quilt. Sew together 20 lime green-and-black units. Make 1 strip, and then sew it to top of quilt. Sew together 20 black-and-red units. Make 1 strip, and then sew it to bottom of quilt.

Border Freedom

If your spiky border comes out too long, simply trim it to fit. If it is too short, add another triangle unit. There are a lot of seams in these borders, and you don't need to take everything apart and start over if the fit isn't perfect. Now is a great time to make do.

To Finish Quilt

To finish quilt, refer to Techniques on pages 16–29, or finish using desired methods.

The quilting on *Limeade* echoes the appliqué designs. Because there is such a sharp, angular look to the border, I wanted soft lines in the quilting to balance the geometry.

Above and right: Contrasting thread makes the quilting stand out, and is perfect for use on the black background.

Round Robin

62" x 62" (157.5 x 157.5 cm)
2005

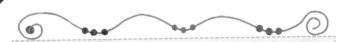

A few years ago I was honored to be included in a Round Robin quilt project with three of the most talented and dear women I know. This was the first time most of us had done a Round Robin, so it was very exciting, challenging, and worrisome all at the same time.

Jean Wells Keenan and Valori Wells Kennedy, owners of the Stitchin' Post in Sisters, Oregon, Betsy Rickles, and I had been talking about doing something like this for a long time. We have all been friends for many years and have admired one another's work. In our Round Robin, each artist began her quilt and then passed it to someone else in the group; once the second quilter contributed her bit, the quilt was passed on again. We had four quilts going at the same time.

We finally pulled it off...well, almost. Valori was to do the final border on my quilt, but decided to have her little girl, Olivia, a month early. We were all so thrilled for her and her growing family—and were so happy that her quilt was finished. It now hangs in Olivia's room.

I had plans to add another border to my quilt, one with all our names on it, so I did that in place of the border that Valori would have done. The pieced sashing on either side of the outer appliqué border was done by Valori, and she had started placing some of the circles on the border when she went into labor. I am so glad to have a little bit of Valori's work in this quilt.

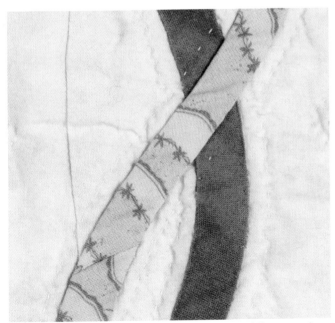

The soft green and gray colors of the vines play beautifully against the neutral background.

Fabric

Note: Yardages are based on fabrics that measure 42" (106.7 cm).

- Neutral background: 3 yards (2.74 meters)
- Blue sawtooth border: 1 yard (.91 meter)
- Vines: ½ yard (.46 meter) each of green and gray fabric
- Red sashing: ½ yard (.46 meter) of one fabric or assorted scrappy strips
- Blue sashing: ¼ yard (.23 meter) of one fabric or assorted scrappy strips
- Flowers, stems, four-patch units, stars, star circles, and letters: fat quarters or large scraps of at least 30 assorted bright, whimsical colors
- Backing: 4 yards (3.66 meters)
- Binding: ⅔ yard (.60 meter)

Materials

- Appliqué thread in various colors
- Basic quilting supplies
- Cotton batting: approximately 68" x 68" (172.7 x 172.7 cm)

To Cut Fabric and Prepare for Appliqué

FROM NEUTRAL BACKGROUND FABRIC:

- Cut 1 square, 24½" (62.3 cm), for center appliqué background.*
- Cut 2 strips, 7" x 23½" (17.8 x 59.7 cm), for side vine-border background strips.
- Cut 2 strips, 7" x 36½" (17.8 x 92.7 cm), for top and bottom vine-border background strips.
- Cut 8 squares, each 2¾" (7 cm), for four-patch corner setting triangles. Cut each square in half diagonally in one direction to yield 2 triangles from each square.
- Cut 8 squares, each 5" (12.7 cm), for four-patch side setting triangles. Cut these in half twice diagonally to yield 4 triangles from each square.

* You will trim this block to measure 23½" x 23½" (59.7 x 59.7 cm) when appliqué is complete and before adding borders.

- Cut 4 strips, 4" x 10" (10.2 x 25.4 cm), for side star background strips.
- Cut 4 strips, 4" x 13½" (10.2 x 34.3 cm), for top and bottom star background strips.
- Cut 6 strips, 6½" (16.5 cm) x width of fabric, for outer appliquéd border.
- Cut 62 squares, each 2⅞" (7.3 cm), for outer sawtooth border.

FROM FLOWER, STEM, FOUR-PATCH, STAR, STAR CIRCLE, AND LETTER FABRICS:

- Cut various flower shapes using templates A–N (pages 112–113).
- Cut assorted bias strips to make stems using ¼" (.6 cm) bias tape maker.
- Cut 80 squares, each 1¾" (4.4 cm), for four-patch units.
- Cut 12 stars using template B (page 112).
- Cut 12 star circles using template F (page 112).
- Cut freehand letters for any names you choose. Letter size is approximately 3½" x 4½" (8.9 x 11.4 cm).

FROM BLUE SAWTOOTH BORDER FABRIC:

- Cut 4 strips, 2" x 23½" (5.1 x 59.7 cm), for first appliquéd sawtooth border.
- Cut 4 strips, 2" x 36½" (5.1 x 92.7 cm), for second appliquéd sawtooth border.
- Cut 62 squares, each 2⅞" (7.3 cm), for outer sawtooth border.

FROM EACH VINE FABRIC:

- Cut enough 1" (2.5 cm)-wide bias strips (for use with ½" (1.3 cm) bias tape maker) to equal approximately 160" (406.4 cm) when sewn together end to end.

FROM BLUE SASHING FABRIC:

- Cut 5 strips, 1¼" (3.2 cm) x width of fabric. *Note:* If you are making pieced sashing, cut enough 1¼" (3.2 cm) strips to equal at least 180" (457.2 cm) when sewn together end to end.

FROM RED SASHING FABRIC:

- Cut 6 strips, 2" (5.1 cm) x width of fabric. *Note:* If you are making pieced sashing, cut enough 2" (5.1 cm) strips to equal at least 240" (609.6 cm) when sewn together end to end.

FROM BINDING FABRIC:

- Cut 7 strips, 2½" (6.4 cm) x width of fabric.

When layering shapes, don't be afraid to hide large portions of some pieces; the results can be stunning.

To Assemble Quilt Top

Note: Use ¼" (.6 cm)-wide seam allowances for all piecing. Press seams as you go. Refer to quilt photo (page 58), How to Appliqué (page 17), and Additional Appliqué Techniques (page 19) as needed.

1. Use compass or large bowl to draw circle in center of 24½" (62.3 cm) neutral center square. Leave plenty of room on all sides for appliqués. Use circle as loose guide for placing flower and stem appliqué shapes.

2. Layer flower and flower stem shapes on marked background. Take photograph of design.

3. Remove top layers of shapes until only bottom layer of appliqué shapes remains. Pin shapes to background and appliqué in place.

4. Repeat until all shapes have been appliquéd to center block.

5. Trim center block to 23½" (59.7 cm) square.

6. With both fabrics right side up, align 2" x 23½" (5.1 x 59.7 cm) blue sawtooth strip along long raw edge of 7" x 23 ½" (17.8 x 59.7 cm) side vine-border background strip. Use large machine stitches to baste pieces together along seam line.

7. Using chalk pencil, mark ¼" (.6 cm) from each short end of blue strip.

8. Mark a line approximately every 2⅜" (7.30 cm) along length of blue strip between marks you drew in step 7. Measure and mark dot at top center of each section. Clip lines to within ½" (1.3 cm) of machine-basted edge.

My love of polka dots is found throughout my appliqué shapes. As seen here, I use circles for flowers, flower centers, and whatever else I can come up with.

9. Needle-turn snipped-edge back using center top mark as guide; also clip and needle-turn first section to make a point. Continue with needle-turn appliqué to make first sawtooth and subsequent sawtooth points down length of strip. Repeat using 2" x 23½" (5.1 x 59.7 cm) blue sawtooth strip and 7" x 23½" (17.8 x 59.7 cm) side vine-border background strip to make second side border.

10. Center remaining 2" x 23½" (5.1 x 59.7 cm) blue sawtooth strip on 7" x 36½" (17.8 x 92.7 cm) vine-border background strip, baste, and repeat steps 6–9 to create top and bottom borders.

11. When appliqué is complete, sew side and then top and bottom vine-background borders to quilt. *Note:* You may need to do a bit of adjusting at the corners.

12. Lightly draw design for gray and green vines on background of borders just added, and then appliqué vines in place.

13. Baste and then appliqué 2" x 36½" (5.1 x 92.7 cm) blue sawtooth strips to outer edges of side, top, and bottom vine-background borders using same technique as described in step 9.

I did not use pre-made templates for the letters, but made my own instead.

14. Using assorted 1¾" (4.4 cm) squares, make 20 four-patch units. Sort units into 4 stacks of 5 units each. Use one stack, 8 neutral side setting triangles, and 4 neutral corner setting triangles to make a row. Trim row to measure 4" x 17½" (10.2 x 44.5 cm), being careful to maintain ¼" (.6 cm) seam allowance on all sides. Make 4 rows.

15. Sew 4" x 10" (10.2 x 25.4 cm) side star background strips to opposite ends of one row from step 14. Make 2 and sew to sides of quilt.

16. Sew 4" x 13½" (10.2 x 34.3 cm) top or bottom star background strips to opposite ends of one row from step 14. Make 2 and sew to top and bottom of quilt.

17. Appliqué 3 star shapes and 3 star center circle shapes in each corner of newly added border.

18. Sew 1¼" (3.2 cm)-wide blue sashing strips together end to end to make one continuous strip. From this strip (or from pieced sashing), cut 2 strips, 43½" (110.5 cm) long for sides, and 2 strips, 45" (114.3 cm) long, for top and bottom. Sew side strips to quilt first, and then sew top and bottom strips to quilt.

19. Sew 6½" (16.5 cm) outer appliqué border strips together end to end to make one continuous strip. From this strip, cut two 45" (114.3 cm)-long strips for sides, and two 57" (144.8 cm)-long strips for top and bottom. Appliqué stems to each border strip, noting that ends of some stems will be sewn into seam.

20. Sew side strips to quilt first, and then sew top and bottom strips to quilt.

21. Appliqué any names or words to newly added border.

I chose to bind the quilt with the same neutral background fabric I used in the center of the quilt. I felt as though I were tying our friendships together.

22. Arrange one small section of flower shapes at a time. Begin by appliquéing bottom-most layer, and add subsequent layers as necessary.

23. Sew 2" (5.1 cm)-wide red sashing strips together end to end to make one long strip. From this strip, cut two 57" (144.8 cm)-long side strips, and two 60" (152.4 cm)-long top and bottom strips. Sew side strips to quilt first, and then sew top and bottom strips to quilt.

24. Refer to Half-Square-Triangle Units (page 25) and Saw-tooth Border (page 27). Using 2⅞" (7.3 cm) neutral squares and 2⅞" (7.3 cm) blue sawtooth squares, make 124 half-square-triangle units. Sew together 30 half-square-triangle units. Make 2 strips, and then sew them to sides of quilt. Sew together 32 half-square-triangle units. Make 2 strips, and then sew them to the top and bottom of the quilt.

To Finish Quilt

To finish quilt, refer to Techniques on pages 16–29, or finish using desired methods.

Heavy crosshatch quilting in the background of the center block sets off the appliqué nicely. Simply quilting around most of the shapes makes them move forward and say, "Look at me!"

I used quilting to repeat the shape of the Four Patch blocks, and—since I love circles so much—I quilted a bunch of them in the final appliqué border to keep the look soft. In a narrow border or sashing, I often lightly mark a wavy line to quilt. Be creative with your quilt designs.

Crosshatch quilting gives weight and interest to the center of the quilt.

Although four artists contributed to this quilt, I think our styles blend together very well.

Frizzles

50" x 56" (127 x 142.2 cm)
2006

Freeform Log-Jammin' blocks have been a design favorite of mine for ages. I have used them in several different ways in many of my quilts. What appeals to me about these blocks is the resulting bits and pieces of color and texture. For some time I had wanted to create a mosaic container, and one day it dawned on me that Log Jammin' blocks would be perfect. I pieced a bunch of blocks, stitched them together, set my template on top of the newly created patchwork fabric, and cut out the desired shape.

After the colorful container was cut, I felt it needed a fairly dramatic background. I auditioned several fabrics, and found a gold that was so rich and wonderful—and complemented the mosaic-style pot nicely.

The "frizzles" (flowers) were inspired by a large-scale leaf-print fabric. Small, dainty flowers would not have worked with this large container. I had a great time drawing my designs on freezer paper and really getting wild and crazy. Since the pot was so powerful, I needed a fabric for the flowers that was different and exciting. I added the small bits of color on the stems to pull the design together.

The appliqué border is all about fun, with a bit of tradition. I love sewing swags, but the end result always seems so fancy. These fun swags are just the right fit.

Fabric

Note: Yardages are based on fabric that measures 42" (106.7 cm) wide.

- Gold background: 2 yards (1.83 meters)
- Black stems and swags: 1 yard (.91 meter)
- Striped border and swag circles: ²/₃ yard (.60 meter)
- "Frizzle" flowers: ¹/₃ yard (.30 meter) each of 2 large-scale prints or 11" x 12" (27.9 x 30.5 cm) scrap for each flower (5)
- Green flowers on swag border: ¹/₃ yard (.30 meter)
- "Frizzle" flower bases: 1 fat quarter
- Vase and stem circles: scraps and strips of at least 15 assorted contrasting fabrics
- Backing: 3 yards (2.74 meters) horizontal seam
- Binding: ¹/₂ yard (.46 meter)

Materials

- Appliqué thread in various colors
- Basic quilting supplies
- Cotton batting: approximately 56" x 62" (142.2 x 157.5 cm)

To Cut Fabric and Prepare for Appliqué

FROM GOLD BACKGROUND FABRIC:

- Cut 1 piece 32½" x 39½" (82.5 x 100.4 cm), for center appliqué background.✻
- Cut 5 strips, 6" (15.2 cm) x width of fabric, for swag border background.

FROM VASE FABRICS:

- Cut multiple strips of varying widths (up to approximately 2" (5.1 cm) wide). If you wish, you can cut as you go.
- Cut 12 stem circles using Stem Circle template (page 115).

FROM BLACK STEMS AND SWAGS FABRIC:

- Cut assorted bias strips to make stems using ¼" (.6 mm) or ½" (1.3 cm) bias tape maker.

✻ You will trim this block to measure 31½" x 38½" (80 x 97.8 cm) when appliqué is complete and before adding borders.

I used the same fabric for all the flower bases; the colors in the fabric match the colors found in the Log Jammin' blocks from which the vase is made.

- Cut 14 border swags using Border Swag template (page 116).
- Cut 4 corner swages using Corner Swag template (page 116).

FROM "FRIZZLE" FLOWER FABRIC(S):

- Cut 5 flowers using Frizzle Flower template (page 115).

FROM "FRIZZLE" FLOWER BASE FABRIC:

- Cut 5 flower bases using Frizzle Flower Base template (page 116).

FROM STRIPED BORDER AND SWAG CIRCLE FABRIC:

- Cut 6 strips, 3½" (8.9 cm) x width of fabric.
- Cut 17 swag circles using Swag Circle template (page 115).

FROM GREEN FLOWER FABRIC:

- Cut 18 swag flowers using Swag Flower template (page 114).

FROM BINDING FABRIC:

- Cut 6 strips, 2½" (6.4 cm) x width of fabric.

To Assemble Quilt Top

Note: Use ¼" (.6 cm)-wide seam allowances for all piecing. Press seams as you go. Refer to quilt photo (page 64), How to Appliqué (page 17), Additional Appliqué Techniques (page 19), and Log Jammin' Block (page 26) as needed.

1. Use assorted fabric scraps and strips to piece enough Log Jammin' blocks to make a piece of fabric approximately 10" x 15" (25.4 x 38.1 cm). From this fabric, cut one vase using Vase template (page 114).

2. Appliqué vase to 32½" x 39½" (82.5 x 100.4 cm) gold background piece, leaving top of vase open for insertion of stems. *Note:* You can also appliqué vase after all stems have been appliquéd.

3. Decide placement of stems and insert stems well inside top of vase. Appliqué stems in place. Appliqué top of vase closed.

4. Position and pin "frizzle" flower and stem circle shapes to background, and then appliqué in place. Repeat with frizzle flower base.

After completing the Log Jammin' blocks, I placed the pot template at an angle to achieve a slightly skewed look.

The flower accents on the swags bring balance to the piece.

5. Trim background to 31½" x 38½" (80 x 97.8 cm).

6. Sew 6" (15.2 cm)-wide gold strips together end to end to make one long strip. From this strip, cut two 38½" (97.8 cm)-long side swag background strips, and two 42½" (108 cm)-long top and bottom swag background strips. Sew side strips to quilt first, then sew top and bottom strips to quilt.

7. Position 4 border swags evenly on each side swag background strip and 3 border swags evenly on top and bottom swag background strips. Place corner swags. Lightly mark placement of swags, and then remove swags.

8. Working one side at a time, appliqué swags.

9. Appliqué swag flowers and swag dots in place on swags.

10. Sew 3½" (8.9 cm)-wide striped border strips together end to end to make one continuous strip. From this strip, cut two 49½" (125.8 cm)-long side border strips, and two 48½" (123.2 cm) top and bottom border strips. Sew side strips to quilt first, and then sew top and bottom strips to quilt.

To Finish Quilt

To finish quilt, refer to Techniques on pages 16–29, or finish using desired methods.

Since this is such a vertical quilt, I added horizontal quilting lines. Notice that the lines continue right up to the swags. To continue the soft lines of the swags, I echoed the shapes with hand quilting.

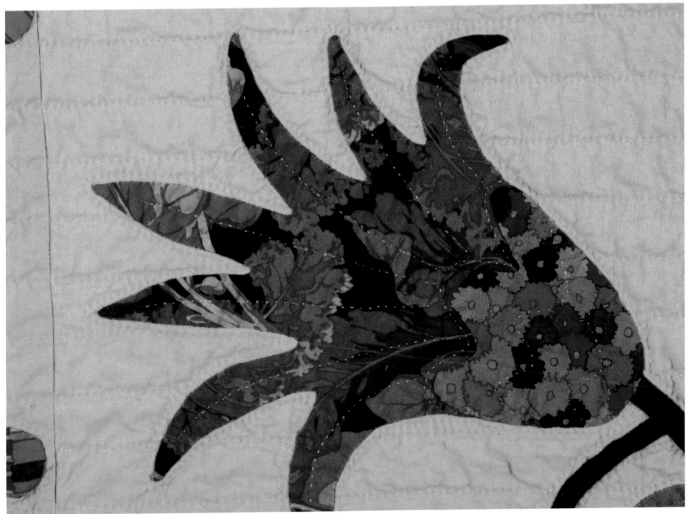

I love the strong design of the flowers. The wild fabric works well with the prints in the pot.

Jammin' with Scarlet

60" x 32" (152.4 x 81.2 cm)
2007

This quilt is a study in richly textured fabric, and in color, shape, and whimsy. I used the bold red fabric to show off the print fabrics in the vases and flowers. You will notice here, as in most of my quilts, the background reads like a solid. I do this in order to get the best possible graphic effect.

My original plan for these blocks was to set them like a four patch, but when I put them together, it just did not feel right. Instead, I laid the blocks out in different ways and settled on the wide horizontal format. I also tried to lengthen the quilt by adding other borders, but nothing seemed to work. Sometimes a new design falls into place right away and other times it takes awhile to get there. Finally, I realized that the quilt was telling me to "stop." The end result is a shape that I had never used before. Making this quilt was a lesson in "less is more."

Fabrics

Note: Yardages are based on fabric that measures 42" (106.7 cm) wide.

- Red background: 2 yards (1.83 meters)
- Purple sashing: ½ yard (.46 meter)
- Lime green sashing and border vine: ½ yard (.46 meter)
- Vases: fat quarter or large scrap each of 4 different fabrics
- Flowers, flower/vine circles, stems, and Log Jammin' blocks: assorted fat quarters and/or assorted scraps
- Backing: 2 yards (1.83 meters)
- Binding: ½ yard (.46 meter)

Materials

- Appliqué thread in various colors
- Basic quilting supplies
- Cotton batting: approximately 38" x 66" (96.5 x 167.6 cm)

The Log Jammin' block side borders add visual weight to the quilt.

To Cut Fabric and Prepare for Appliqué

FROM RED BACKGROUND FABRIC:

- Cut 4 pieces, 13" x 22½" (33 x 57.2 cm), for block backgrounds.*
- Cut 3 strips, 4½" (11.4 cm) x width of fabric, for top and bottom borders.

FROM EACH VASE FABRIC:

- Cut 1 vase using Vase template (page 117).

FROM FLOWER, FLOWER/VINE DOT, STEM, AND LOG JAMMIN' BLOCK FABRICS:

- Cut assorted bias strips to make stems using ¼" (.6 cm) bias tape maker.
- Cut assorted vine circles and flower circles shapes using templates A–H (page 118).
- Cut multiple strips of varying widths up to approximately 2" (5.1 cm) wide, for Log Jammin' blocks. If you wish, you can cut as you go.

* You will trim each block to measure 12" x 21½" (30.5 x 54.6 cm) when appliqué is complete and before adding sashing and borders

FROM PURPLE SASHING FABRIC:

- Cut 3 strips, 1½" (3.8 cm) x width of fabric, for horizontal sashing.
- Cut 3 strips, 1½" (3.8 cm) x width of fabric, for checkerboard sashing.

FROM LIME GREEN SASHING AND VINE FABRIC:

- Cut 3 strips, 1½" (3.8 cm) x width of fabric, for checkerboard sashing.
- Cut enough bias strips for use with ¼" (.6 cm) bias tape maker to equal approximately 150" (381 cm). *Note:* It is difficult to pull seamed strips through a ¼" (.6 cm) bias tape maker. For this quilt, do not sew strips together. Instead, cover each raw end with an appliquéd circle or needle-turn the ends.

FROM BINDING FABRIC:

- Cut 5 strips, 2½" (6.4 cm) x width of fabric.

To Assemble Quilt Top

Note: Use ¼" (.6 cm)-wide seam allowances for all piecing. Press seams as you go. Refer to quilt photo (page 68), How to Appliqué (page 17), and Additional Appliqué Techniques (page 19) as needed.

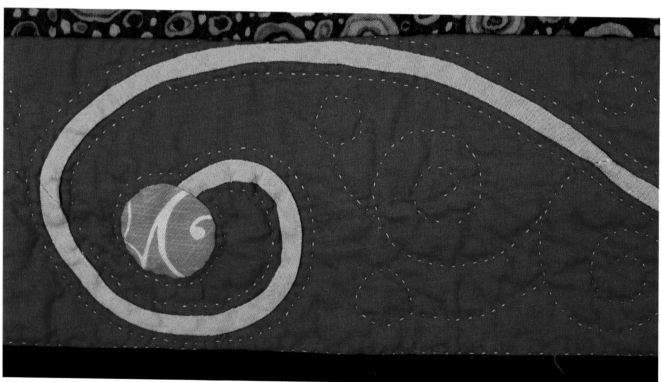

Red background fabric really shows off the appliquéd vines and circles.

QUILT CENTER:

1. Position vase, stem, flower, and flower circle shapes on each 13" x 22½" (33 x 57.2 cm) red background block to preview how the blocks will look together. Lightly draw guidelines for stems. Take note of top of each vase, and allow plenty of extra length when cutting stems. *Note:* You will lose a bit as you turn under edges of vase and flowers; be sure to compensate.

2. Appliqué stems, and then the vases, flowers, and flower circles in place.

3. Trim each block to 12" x 21½" (30.5 x 54.6 cm).

CHECKERED SASHING:

Note: This sashing can be cut from preprinted checked fabric or you can make your own checkerboard fabric as I have. I used the same strip-piecing method typically used for making multiple Nine-Patch blocks.

1. Sew 1½" (3.8 cm)-wide lime green strip between two 1½" (3.8 cm)-wide purple strips (Unit A). Sew 1½" (3.8 cm)-wide purple strip between two 1½" (3.8 cm)-wide lime green strips (Unit B).

2. Cut 20 segments, each 1½" (3.8 cm) wide, from Unit A. Cut 15 segments, each 1½" (3.8 cm) wide, from Unit B.

3. Beginning and ending with Unit A segment, alternate and sew together 4 Unit A segments and 3 Unit B segments. Make 5 sashing strips.

4. Beginning and ending with a sashing strip from step 3, alternate and sew together appliquéd blocks and 5 sashing strips to make a horizontal row.

LOG JAMMIN' BLOCKS

1. Refer to Log Jammin' Block (page 26) as needed and use assorted strips to make 18 Log Jammin' blocks.

2. Trim each block to measure 4½" x 4½" (11.4 x 11.4 cm).

3. Sew 5 blocks together to create a vertical strip. Make 2 and sew to opposite short sides of quilt. Set remaining blocks aside for now. *Note:* These strips may come up a bit short. Don't worry; just sew on an additional strip or two as needed so strip measures 21½" (54.6 cm) long.

I used both outline and straight-line quilting in each block.

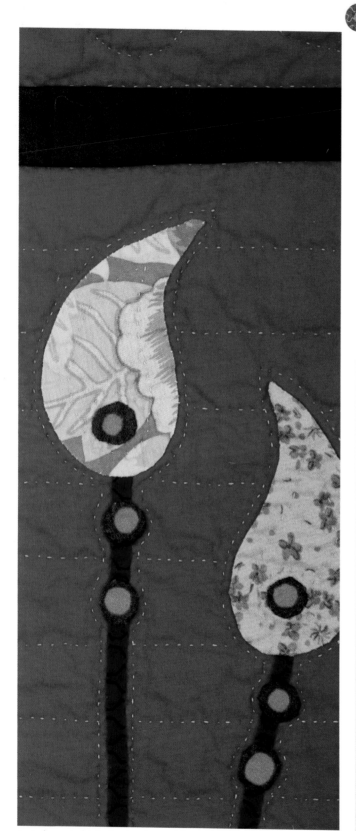

PURPLE SASHING:

Sew 1½" (3.8 cm)-wide purple sashing strips together end to end to make one long strip. From this strip, cut two 59½" (151.2 cm)-long strips. Sew one strip to top and one strip to bottom of quilt.

TOP AND BOTTOM BORDERS:

1. Sew three 4½" (11.4 cm)-wide red strips together end to end to make one long strip. From this strip, cut two 43 ½" (110.5 cm)-long strips.

2. Sew two remaining Log Jammin' blocks to opposite short ends of each strip from step 1. Sew one strip to top and one strip to bottom of quilt.

3. Lightly draw guideline for placement of lime green vines. Pin and appliqué vines, and then vine circles, in place.

Finishing the Quilt

To finish quilt, refer to Techniques on pages 16–29, or finish using desired methods.

To emphasize the vases and flowers, I outlined each shape with quilting.

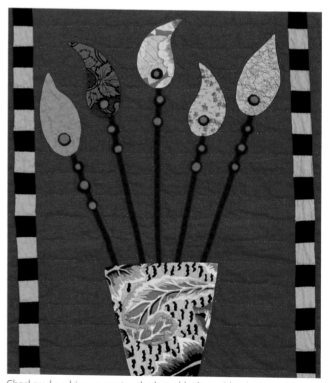

I used purple fabric for the vine and flower dots in order to tie the various elements of the quilt together—notice how purple fabric was also used in the sashing.

Checkered sashing separates the large blocks and lends the quilt a quirky look.

Dozens of Baskets

36" x 36" (91.4 x 91.4 cm)
2006

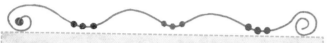

If you are looking for a playful, simple, graphic project that also uses up lots of scraps, this is the one for you. The technique I used to make the basket block is quick and easy. Each basket is just a half-square-triangle unit with a handle attached. As you play around with the block placement, notice the secondary designs that appear.

Fabric

Note: Yardages are based on fabric that measures 42" (106.7 cm) wide.

- Muslin: ¾ yard (.69 meter)
- Polka-dot outer border: ½ yard (.46 meter)
- Basket base and handle: scraps of 18 assorted fabrics
  Note: Each fabric makes 2 baskets.
- Black center square: 1½" (3.8 cm) square
- Backing: 1¼ yards (1.14 meters)
- Binding: ½ yard (.46 meter)

Materials

- Appliqué thread in various colors
- Basic quilting supplies
- Cotton batting: approximately 42" x 42" (106.7 x 106.7 cm)

To Cut Fabric and Prepare for Appliqué

FROM EACH BASKET FABRIC:

- Cut 1 square, 4⅞" (12.4 cm), for basket bases. Cut square in half diagonally in one direction to yield 2 triangles.
- Cut 2 basket handles using Dozens of Baskets Handle template (page 119).

FROM MUSLIN:

- Cut 18 squares, each 4⅞" (12.4 cm), for handle backgrounds. Cut each square in half diagonally in one direction to yield 2 triangles from each square.
- Cut 4 strips, 1½" x 12½" (3.8 x 31.8 cm), for sashing.
- Cut 2 strips, 2½" x 25½" (6.4 x 64.8 cm), for side inner borders.
- Cut 2 strips, 2½" x 29½" (6.4 x 75 cm), for top and bottom inner borders.

FROM POLKA-DOT OUTER BORDER FABRIC:

- Cut 2 strips, 3½" x 29½" (8.9 x 75 cm), for side outer borders.
- Cut 2 strips, 3½" x 35½" (8.9 x 90.2 cm), for top and bottom outer borders.

FROM BINDING FABRIC:

- Cut 4 strips, 2½" (6.4 cm) x width of fabric.

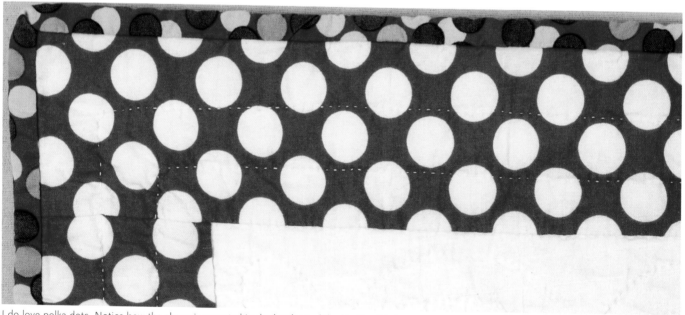

I do love polka dots. Notice how the shape is repeated in the border and the binding fabrics.

To Assemble Quilt Top

Note: Use ¼" (.6 cm)-wide seam allowances for all piecing. Press seams as you go. Refer to quilt photo (page 73), How to Appliqué (page 17), Additional Appliqué Techniques (page 19), and Half-Square-Triangle Units (page 25) as needed.

1. Appliqué one handle to each muslin triangle, carefully lining up bottom of handle with bias edge of triangle.

2. Sew each appliquéd triangle from step 1 to matching basket triangle along bias edge.

3. Arrange blocks to your liking in 3 rows of 3 blocks each. Sew blocks together into rows, and then sew rows together. Make 4 large blocks.

4. Sew 1½" x 12½" (3.8 x 31.8 cm) sashing strip between 2 large blocks from step 3. Make 2.

5. Sew 1½" x 12½" (3.8 x 31.8 cm) sashing strip to opposite sides of 1½" (3.8 cm) black square. Sew this pieced sashing strip between units from step 4, carefully lining up center seams.

6. Sew 2½" x 25½" (6.4 x 64.8 cm) muslin inner-border strips to sides of quilt, and then 2½" x 29½" (6.4 x 75 cm) muslin inner-border strips to top and bottom.

7. Sew 3½" x 29½" (8.9 x 75 cm) polka-dot outer-border strips to sides of quilt, and then 3½" x 35½" (8.9 x 90.2 cm) polka-dot outer-border strips to top and bottom.

To Finish Quilt

To finish quilt, refer to Techniques on pages 16–29, or finish using desired methods.

For the quilting design, I simply drew a squiggly line in the sashing, and then drew some swag shapes in the muslin inner border. Notice the circle quilted into the basket base—this goes nicely with the polka-dot border.

Sometimes the most important design elements are the smallest ones. Here, a little black square lends a sense of balance to the design.

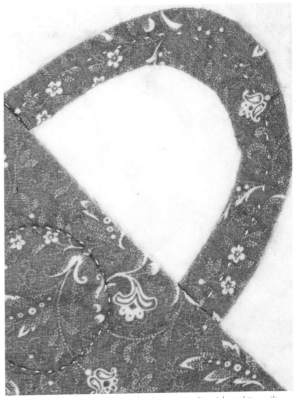

The basket handles are the only shapes appliquéd to this quilt. The basket body is one-half of a half-square-triangle block.

CHAPTER FOUR

PICTURE FRAME QUILTS

A few years ago, I began experimenting with simple, small appliqué designs. I made some quilts with the intention of having them framed. About the same time, my husband opened a small factory in China to manufacture climbing equipment. While researching factories there, he made contact with a wonderful gentleman named Li Guohua in Yantai City.

As my husband's knowledge of Chinese manufacturing and contacts grew, he encouraged me to have my small quilts reproduced in China. Guohua's wife, Wang, is also very involved in the business, and through her and her husband, we met Mu, who has a business making high-end bedding for hotels in China. Through these terrific people and their extended families, I have had some of my work reproduced overseas. Wang's cousin, also named Wang, does most of the sewing, though some of her fellow villagers work on larger orders. The small quilt projects in this chapter feature reproductions of my original designs done by my friends in China.

This series of small container quilts is reproduced by my friends in China.

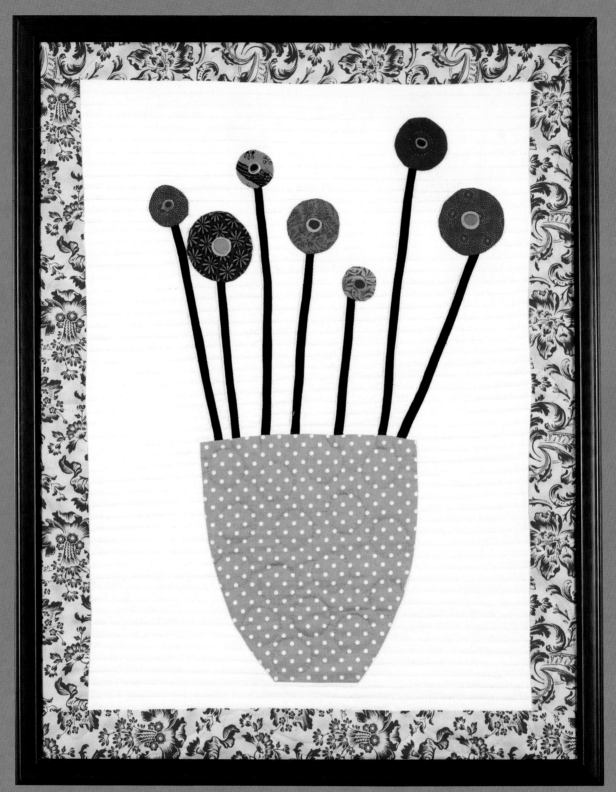

Polka Dot Pot I

28" x 36" (71.1 x 91.4 cm) framed
2005

How can anyone resist the incredible variety of colorful, crazy, and wild polka-dot fabrics now available? You may want to make several of these pots just so you can use all the different dots. This particular design is great for anyone just starting his or her appliqué journey. A more experienced quilter may enjoy this as a quick and simple take-along project.

Fabrics

Note: Yardages are based on fabric that measures 42" (106.7 cm) wide.

- Muslin: ⅔ yard (.60 meter)
- Border print: ½ yard (.46 meter)
- Polka dot pot: 1 fat quarter or 11" x 12" (27.9 x 30.5 cm) scrap
- Stems: ⅛ yard (.11 meter) or multiple scraps
- Circle flowers and flower centers: assorted scraps
- Backing: 1 yard (.91 meter)
- Binding: ⅓ yard (.30 meter)

Materials

- Appliqué thread in various colors
- Basic quilting supplies
- Cotton batting: approximately 32" x 40" (81.2 x 101.6 cm)

To Cut Fabric and Prepare for Appliqué

FROM MUSLIN:
- Cut 1 piece, 19½" x 27½" (49.6 x 69.9 cm), for appliqué background.*

FROM POLKA-DOT POT FABRIC:
- Cut 1 pot using Pot I template (page 121).

FROM STEM FABRIC:
- Cut 7 bias strips of varying lengths to make stems using ¼" (.6 cm) or ½" (1.3 cm) bias tape maker.

FROM CIRCLE FLOWER AND FLOWER CENTER FABRICS:
- Cut 1 of each shape using templates A–N (page 120).

FROM BORDER PRINT:
- Cut 2 strips, 4" x 26½" (10.2 x 67.3 cm), for side borders.
- Cut 2 strips, 4" x 25½" (10.2 x 64.8 cm), for top and bottom borders.

* You will trim this block to measure 18½" x 26½" (47 x 67.3 cm) when appliqué is complete and before adding borders.

The border fabric mimics a picture mat, and looks great in a frame.

To Assemble Quilt Top

Note: Use ¼" (.6 cm)-wide seam allowances for all piecing. Press seams as you go. Refer to quilt photo (page 78), How to Appliqué (page 17), and Additional Appliqué Techniques (page 19) as needed.

1. Position pot on background. Lightly draw guidelines for stem placement, and then position stems.

2. Remove pot and all but one stem. Appliqué stem and then position, pin, and appliqué rest of stems, one at a time. Because bottoms of stems will be covered by pot, they do not need to be appliquéd.

3. Re-position pot to cover bottom of stems, pin to background, and appliqué in place.

4. Appliqué flowers and then flower centers to quilt.

5. Trim block to 18½" x 26½" (47 x 67.3 cm).

6. Sew 4" x 26½" (10.2 x 67.3 cm) borders to sides of quilt. Sew 4" x 25½" (10.2 x 64.8 cm) borders to top and bottom of quilt.

To Finish Quilt

To finish quilt, refer to Techniques on pages 16–29, or finish using desired methods. If you plan to frame quilt, do not bind it.

The fabric that inspired the name of the quilt is, of course, polka dots.

This simple appliqué design is a great "take-along" piece. Its small size lets you work on it practically anywhere.

Polka Dot Pot II

28" x 36" (71.1 x 91.4 cm) framed
2005

*P*olka Dot Pot II is a perfect complement to *Polka Dot Pot I* (page 78), but it is a little bit more involved. Once you have mastered *Polka Dot Pot I*, though, this quilt should be easy. Based on a classic topiary shape, this design could be done many ways. Think about creating a topiary with more than one ball of flowers. This would require more work, but can't you just see it hanging on a tall, narrow wall?

Fabrics

Note: Yardages are based on fabric that measures 42" (106.7 cm) wide.

- Muslin: ²⁄₃ yard (.60 meter)
- Border print: ¹⁄₂ yard (.46 meter)
- Polka dot pot: 7¹⁄₂" (19.1 cm) square
- Stem: 1¹⁄₂" x 9¹⁄₂" (3.8 x 24.2 cm) strip
- Flowers: assorted colorful scraps
- Backing: 1 yard (.91 meter)
- Binding: ¹⁄₃ yard (.30 meter)

Materials

- Appliqué thread in various colors
- Basic quilting supplies
- Cotton batting: approximately 32" x 40" (81.2 x 101.6 cm)

Make sure to cover the base of the topiary stem completely before appliquéing the pot in place.

Pull one of the colors from the flowers to frame the quilt.

To Cut Fabric and Prepare for Appliqué

FROM MUSLIN:

- Cut 1 piece, 19¹⁄₂" x 27¹⁄₂" (49.6 x 69.9 cm), for appliqué background.*

FROM FLOWER FABRICS:

- Cut several of each shape using templates A–N (pages 112–113). Make sure you have lots of color and contrast.

FROM BORDER PRINT:

- Cut 2 strips, 4" x 26¹⁄₂" (10.2 x 67.3 cm), for side borders.
- Cut 2 strips, 4" x 25¹⁄₂" (10.2 x 64.8 cm), for top and bottom borders.

* You will trim this block to measure 18¹⁄₂" x 26¹⁄₂" (47 x 67.3 cm) when appliqué is complete and before adding borders.

To Assemble Quilt Top

Note: Use ¼" (.6 cm)-wide seam allowances for all piecing. Press seams as you go. Refer to quilt photo (page 81), How to Appliqué (page 17), and Additional Appliqué Techniques (page 19) as needed.

1. Position pot and stem on background. Pin stem, remove pot, and then appliqué stem in place.

2. Re-position pot to cover bottom of stem, pin to background, and appliqué in place.

3. Layer flower shapes on background. Take photograph of design.

4. Remove top layers of shapes until only bottom layer of appliqué shapes remain. Pin shapes to background and appliqué in place.

5. Repeat until all shapes have been appliquéd to center block.

6. Trim muslin block to 18½" x 26½" (47 x 67.3 cm).

7. Sew 4" x 26½" (10.2 x 67.3 cm) borders to sides of quilt. Sew 4" x 25½" (10.2 x 64.8 cm) borders to top and bottom of quilt.

To Finish Quilt

To finish quilt, refer to Techniques on pages 16–29, or finish using desired methods. If you plan to frame quilt, do not bind it.

I used the same flower shapes that I used in *Round Robin* (page 58). Never be afraid to repeat design elements that work successfully in your quilts.

I often use horizontal straight line quilting to offset a vertical piece.

Retro Bag

8" x 10" (20.3 x 25.4 cm) framed
2004

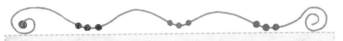

I love the contemporary shape and style of this bag. Because I usually work with so many circles, it was nice to mix it up and do a few squares for a change. This design would also be great in a larger quilt, with lots of different-colored fabrics and textures.

Fabric

Note: Yardages are based on fabric that measures 42" (106.7 cm) wide.

- Background: 10" x 12" (25.4 x 30.5 cm) piece
- Bag base: 6" (15.2 cm) square
- Bag squares: 1 fat quarter
- Handle: 6" (15.2 cm) square
- Circles: 2 small, different-colored scraps

Materials

- Appliqué thread in various colors
- Basic quilting supplies
- Cotton batting: approximately 14" x 16" (35.6 x 40.6 cm)

To Cut Fabric and Prepare for Appliqué

FROM BAG SQUARE FABRIC:

- Cut 9 shapes, using Square template (page 119).

FROM HANDLE FABRIC:

- Cut 1 handle using Handle template (page 119).

FROM CIRCLE FABRICS:

- Cut 2 circles total, 1 using Small Circle template and 1 using Large Circle template (page 119).

To Assemble Quilt Top

Note: Refer to quilt photo (page 84), How to Appliqué (page 17), and Additional Appliqué Techniques (page 19) as needed.

1. Position bag base, bag handle, and circles on background.

2. Remove all shapes except handle. Pin and appliqué handle to background.

3. Re-position bag base, taking care to fully cover base of handle with room for needle-turned seam allowance. Pin and appliqué bag base to background.

4. Position, pin, and appliqué 9 bag squares on bag base.

5. Re-position, pin, and appliqué circles inside handle.

To Finish Quilt

To finish quilt, refer to Techniques on pages 16–29. You do not need a backing, nor do you need to bind quilt for framing. You may need to trim quilt for it to fit comfortably within frame, without excess bulk.

I used outline quilting to emphasize the appliqué shapes on this quilt.

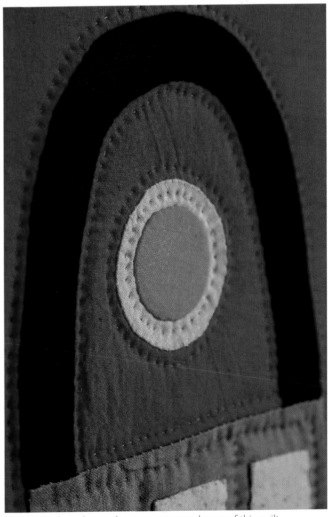

The bold colors play up the contemporary shapes of this quilt.

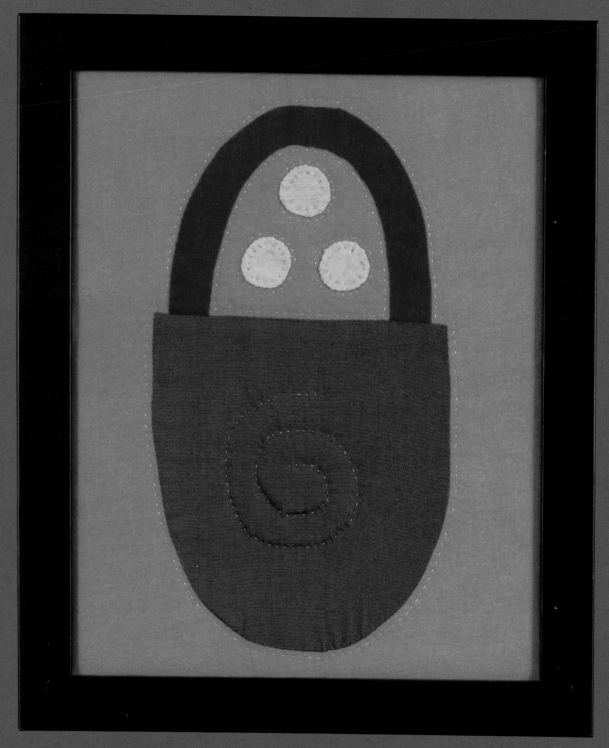

Green Peas

8" x 10" (20.3 x 25.4 cm) framed
2004

The electric orange background of this quilt will surely brighten anyone's day. This simple, bold design is perfect for a small quilt.

Fabric

Note: Yardages are based on fabric that measures 42" (106.7 cm) wide.

- Background: 10" x 12" (25.4 x 30.5 cm) piece
- Basket: 6" x 7" (15.2 x 17.8 cm) piece
- Handle: 6" (15.2 cm) square
- Green peas: small scraps

Materials

- Appliqué thread in various colors
- Basic quilting supplies
- Cotton batting: approximately 14" x 16" (35.6 x 40.6 cm)

To Cut Fabric and Prepare for Appliqué

FROM BASKET FABRIC:

- Cut 1 basket using Basket template (page 122).

FROM HANDLE FABRIC:

- Cut 1 handle using Handle template (page 122).

FROM GREEN PEA FABRIC:

- Cut 3 peas using Green Pea template (page 122).

To Assemble Quilt Top

Note: Refer to quilt photo (page 86), How to Appliqué (page 17), and Additional Appliqué Techniques (page 19) as needed.

1. Position all shapes on background to audition fabric.

2. Remove all shapes except handle. Pin and appliqué handle to background.

3. Re-position basket, taking care to fully cover base of handle with room for needle-turned seam allowance. Pin and appliqué basket to background.

4. Appliqué peas inside handle.

To Finish Quilt

To finish quilt, refer to Techniques on pages 16–29. You do not need a backing, nor do you need to bind the quilt for framing. You may need to trim quilt for it to fit comfortably within a frame, without excess bulk.

I used outline quilting to emphasize the appliqué shapes on this quilt.

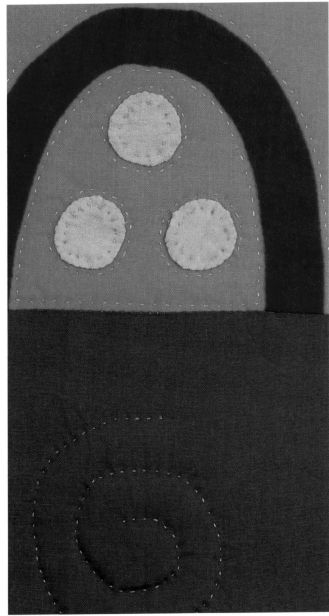

Though the quilting on my small quilt is simple, feel free to add more quilt designs as desired.

Blueberries

8" x 10" (20.3 x 25.4 cm) framed
2004

I never get tired of this classic basket shape. Whether it is pieced by machine, or hand appliquéd like this one, the motif is always a head turner. For some reason, almost everyone is drawn to this simple basket.

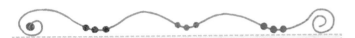

Fabric

Note: Yardages are based on fabric that measures 42" (106.7 cm) wide.

- Background: 10" x 12" (25.4 x 30.5 cm) piece
- Basket body: 6" x 8" (15.2 x 20.3 cm) scrap
- Basket base: 5" (12.7 cm) square
- Handle: 6" (15.2 cm) square
- Blueberries: small scraps

Materials

- Appliqué thread in various colors
- Basic quilting supplies
- Cotton batting: approximately 14" x 16" (35.6 x 40.6 cm)

To Cut Fabrics and Prepare for Appliqué

FROM BASKET BODY FABRIC:

- Cut 1 basket body using Basket Body template (page 123).

FROM BASKET BASE FABRIC:

- Cut 1 basket base using Basket Base template (page 123).

FROM HANDLE FABRIC:

- Cut 1 handle using Handle template (page 123).

FROM BLUEBERRIES FABRIC:

- Cut 3 blueberries using Blueberry template (page 123).

To Assemble Quilt Top

Note: Use ¼" (.6 cm)-wide seam allowances for all piecing. Press seams as you go. Refer to quilt photo (page 88), How to Appliqué (page 17), and Additional Appliqué Techniques (page 19) as needed.

1. Position all shapes on background to audition fabric.
2. Remove all shapes except handle. Pin and appliqué handle to background.
3. Re-center basket base and body, and then remove basket body. Pin and appliqué basket base to background.
4. Position basket body, taking care to fully cover base of handle with room for needle-turned seam allowance. Pin and appliqué basket body to background.
5. Appliqué blueberries inside handle.

To Finish Quilt

To finish quilt, refer to Techniques on pages 16–29. You do not need a backing, nor do you need to bind quilt for framing. You may need to trim quilt for it to fit comfortably within a frame, without excess bulk.

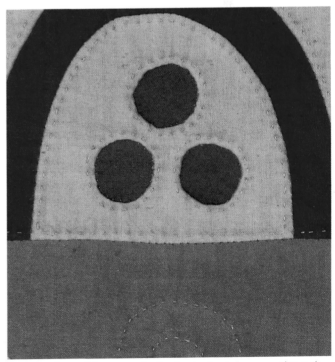

I used outline quilting to emphasize the appliqué shapes on this quilt.

CHAPTER FIVE

TEMPLATES

Opposite: The *Window Box* quilt was inspired by my love of window boxes. This is how I wish my window boxes *really* looked.

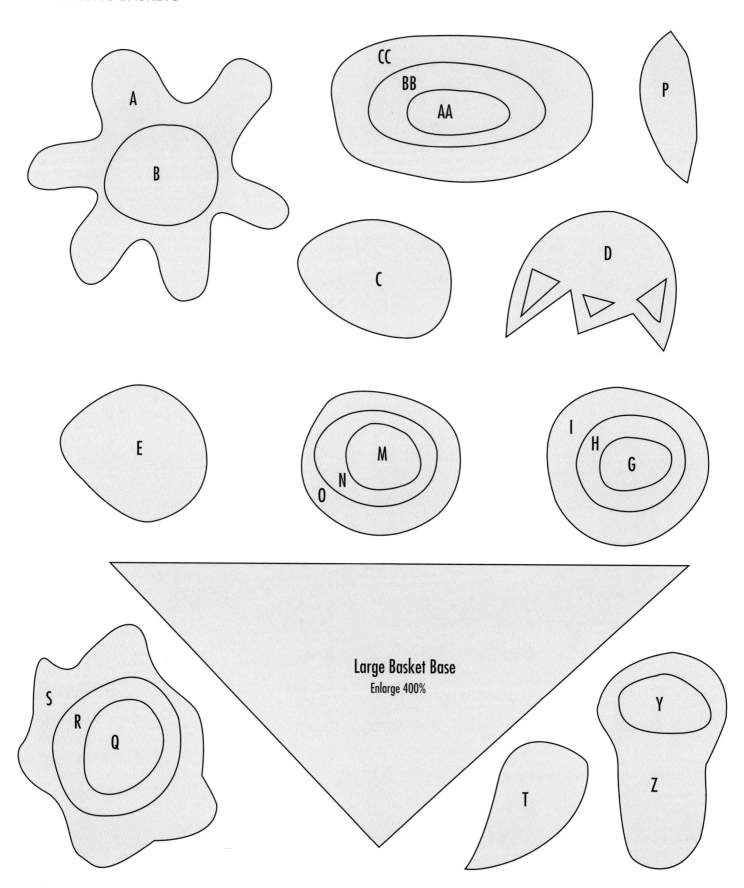

A

B

CC

BB

AA

P

C

D

E

I

H

G

M

N

O

Large Basket Base
Enlarge 400%

S

R

Q

Y

Z

T

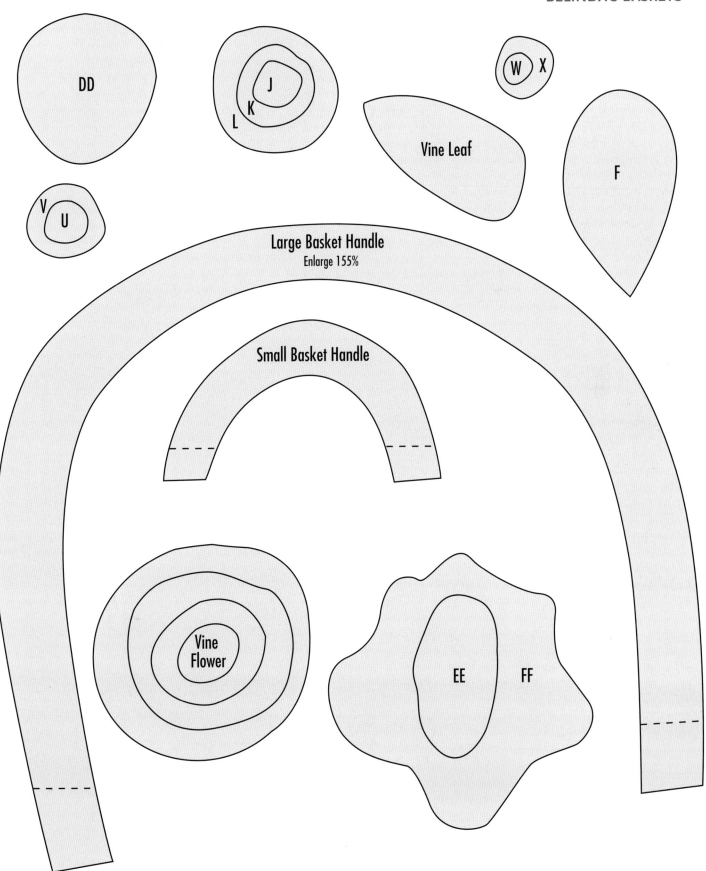

DD

J

K

L

Vine Leaf

W X

F

V U

Large Basket Handle
Enlarge 155%

Small Basket Handle

Vine
Flower

EE FF

Golden Goblet

Enlarge 250%

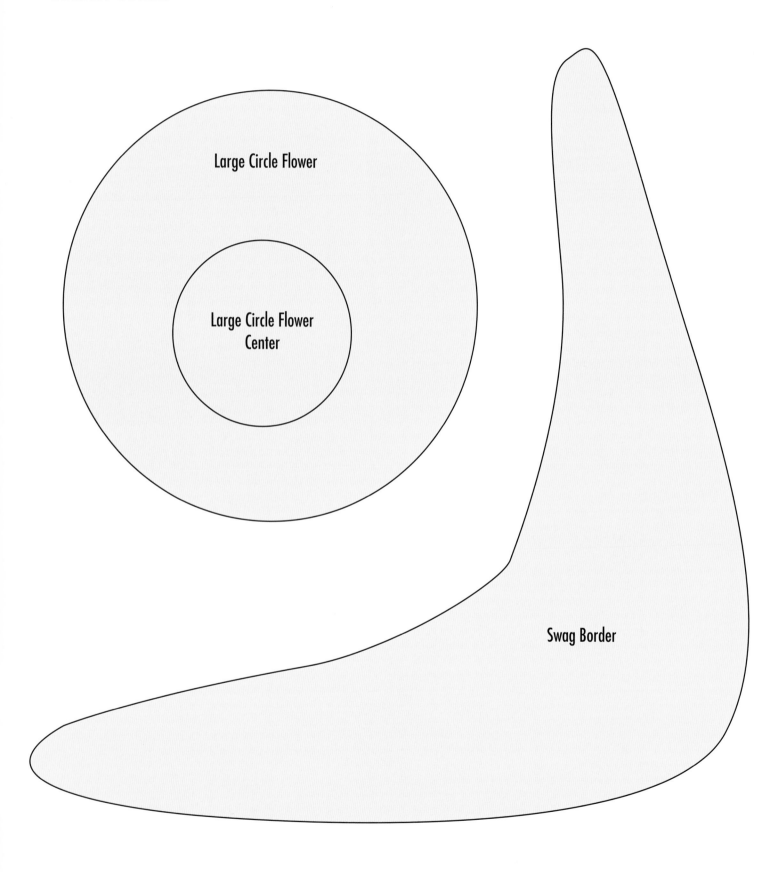

Large Circle Flower

Large Circle Flower
Center

Swag Border

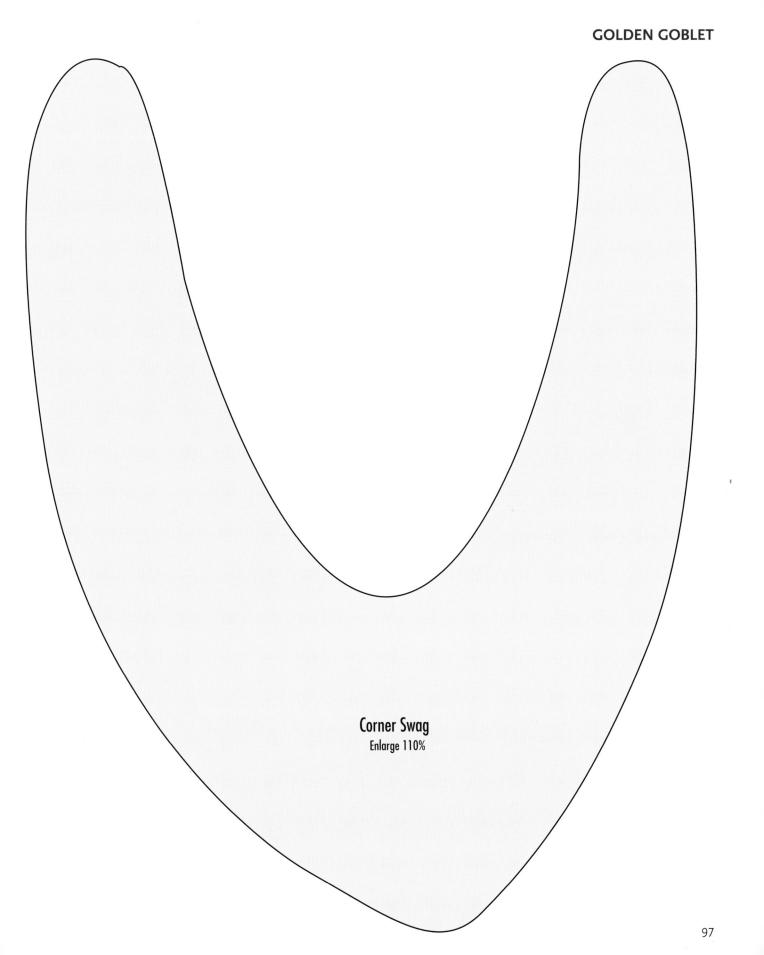

Corner Swag
Enlarge 110%

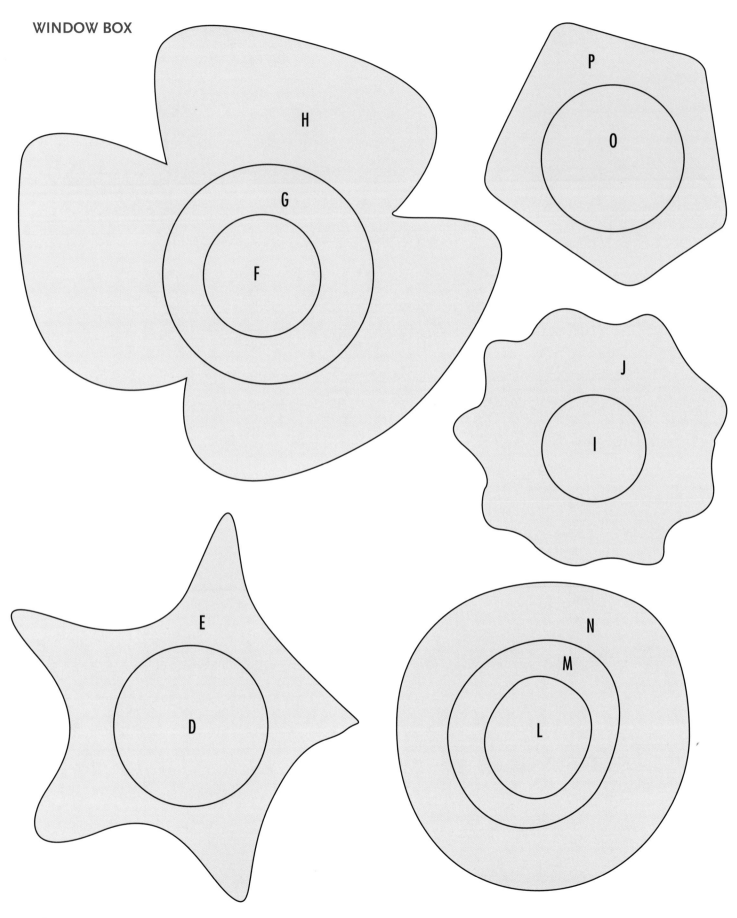

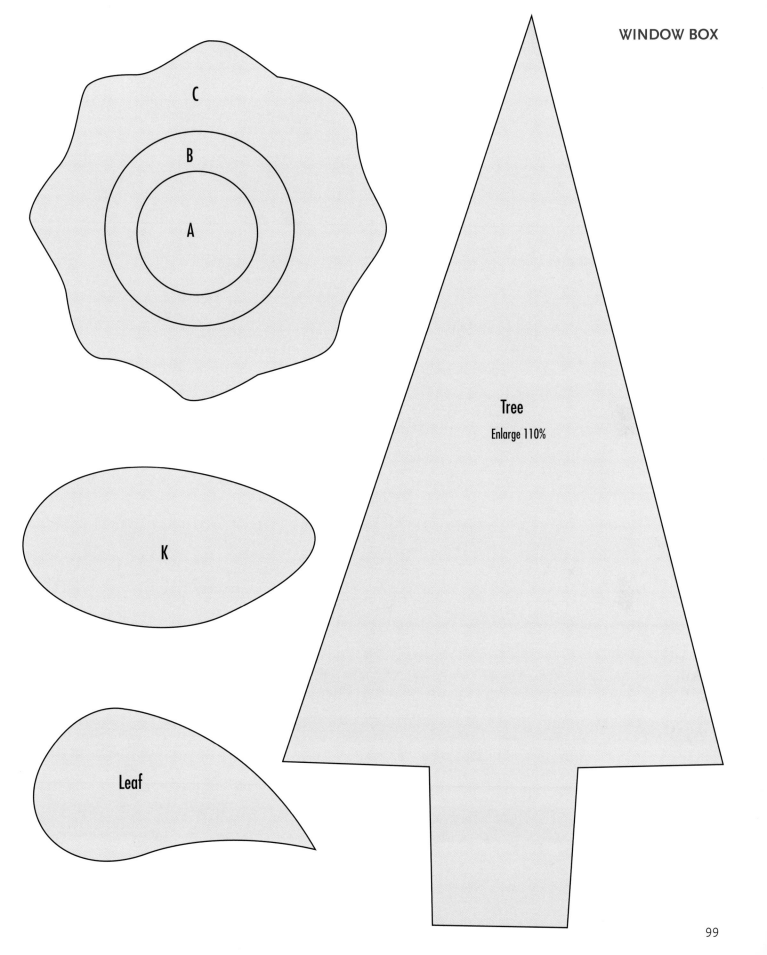

C

B

A

K

Leaf

Tree

Enlarge 110%

Heirloom Rose

Vase
Enlarge 165%

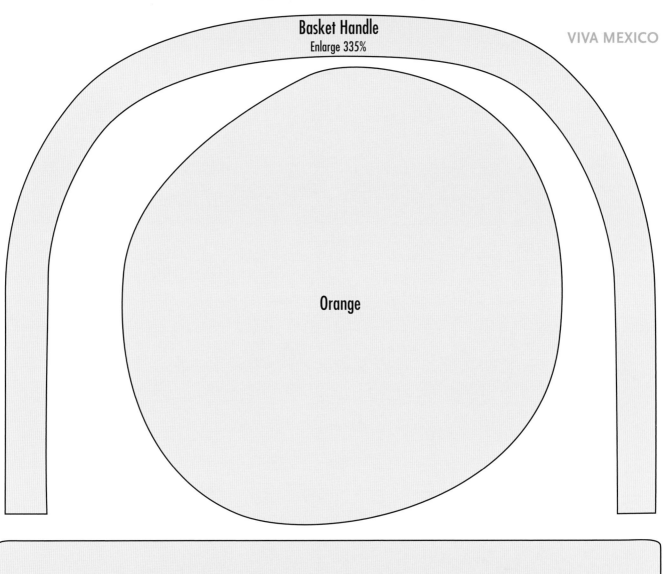

Basket Handle
Enlarge 335%

Orange

Basket Base
Enlarge 335%

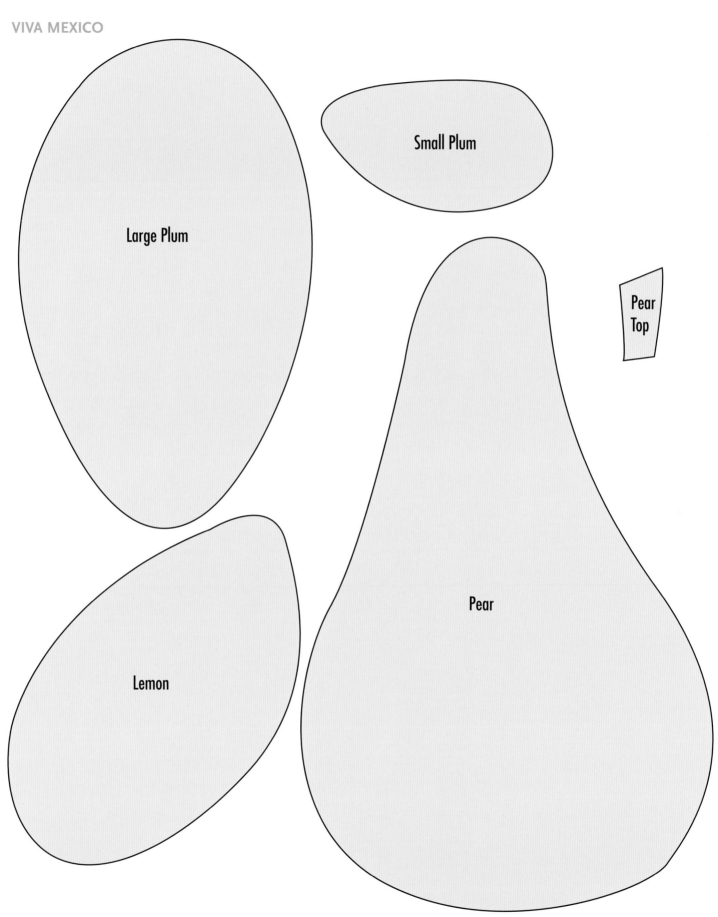

Large Plum

Small Plum

Pear Top

Lemon

Pear

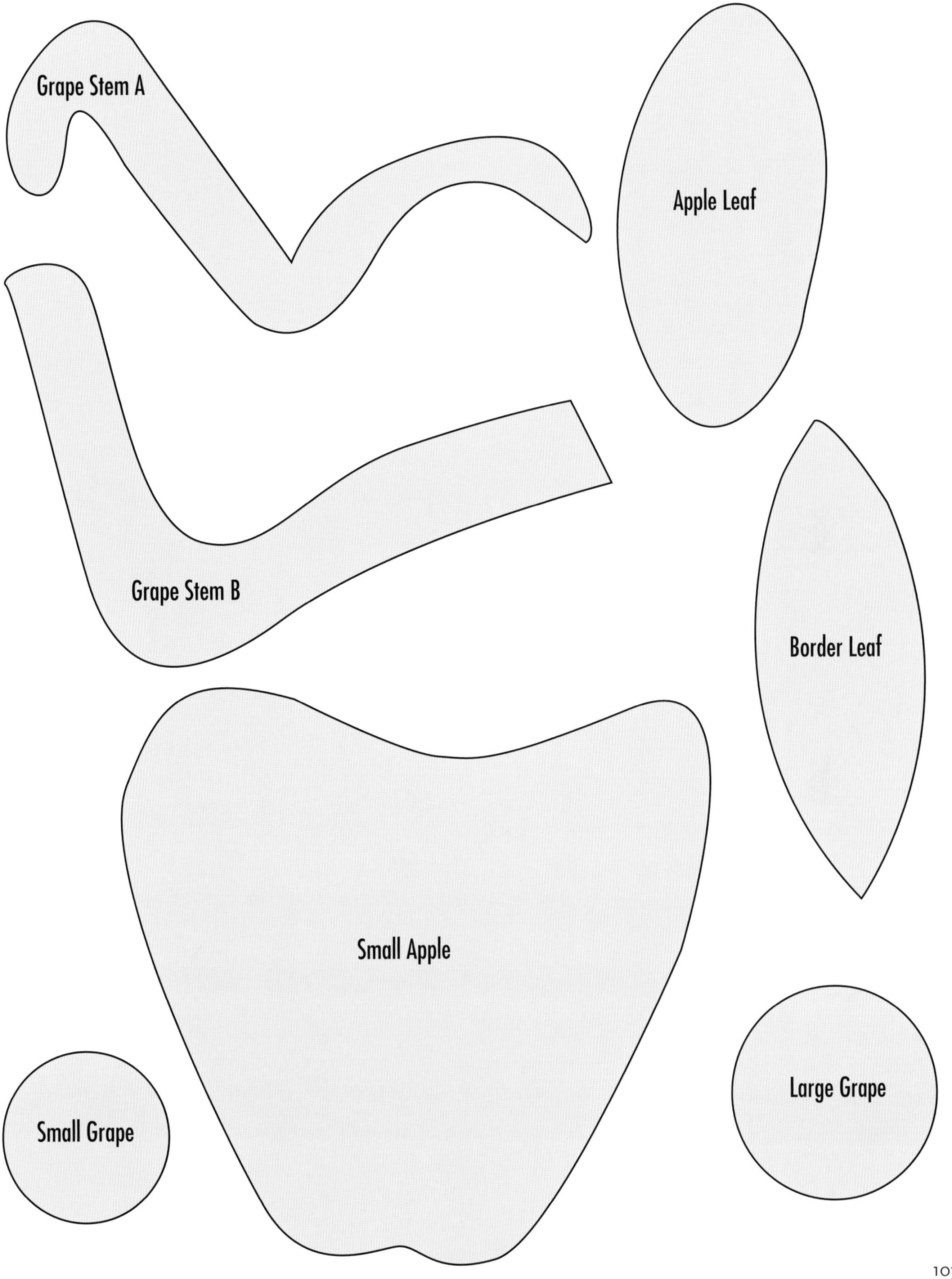

Grape Stem A

Apple Leaf

Border Leaf

Grape Stem B

Small Apple

Small Grape

Large Grape

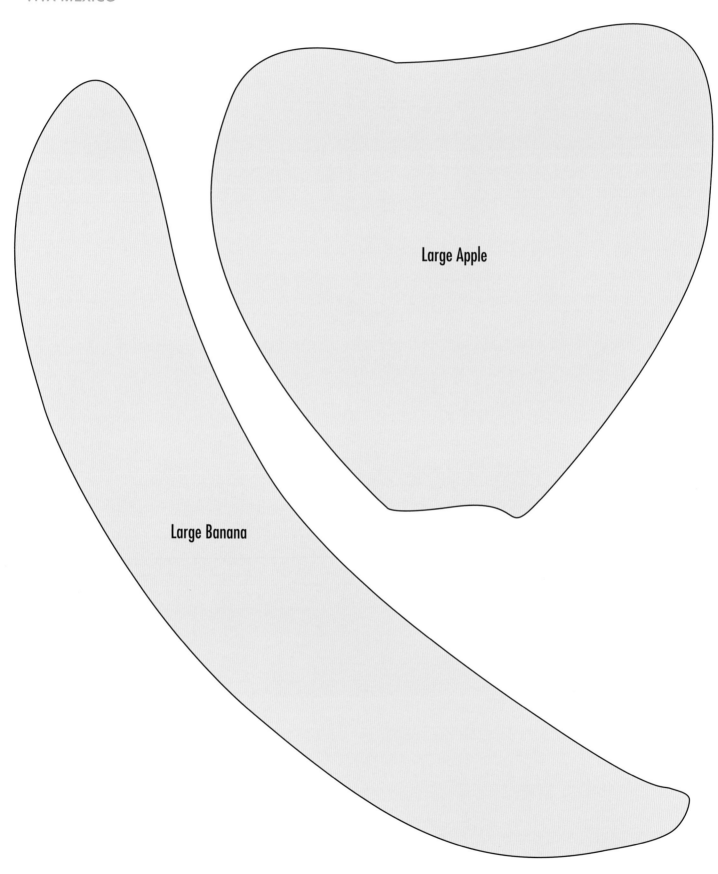

Large Apple

Large Banana

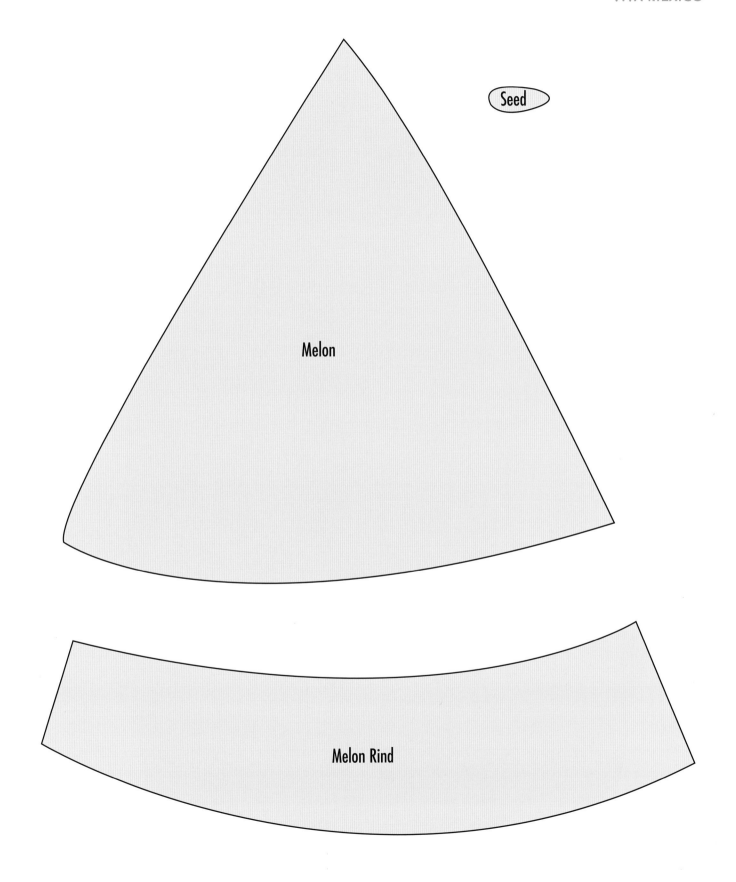

Seed

Melon

Melon Rind

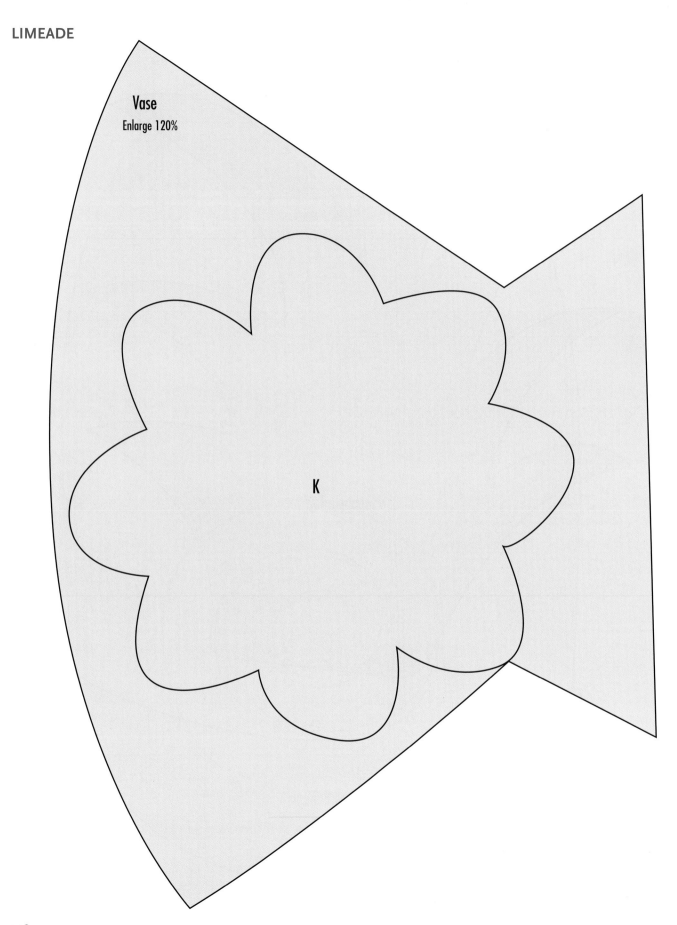

Vase
Enlarge 120%

K

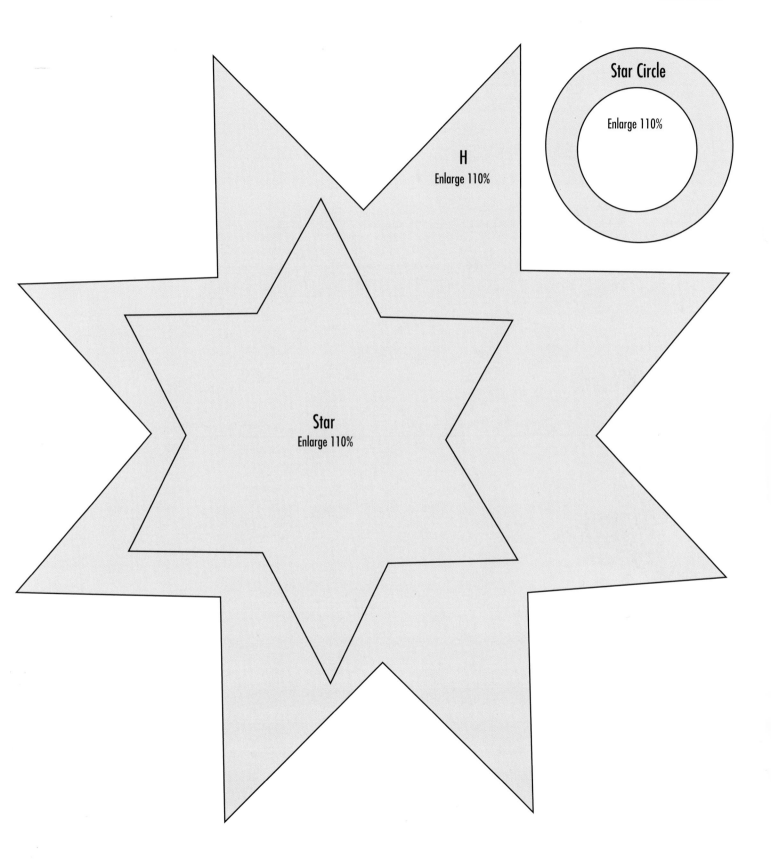

Star Circle

Enlarge 110%

H
Enlarge 110%

Star
Enlarge 110%

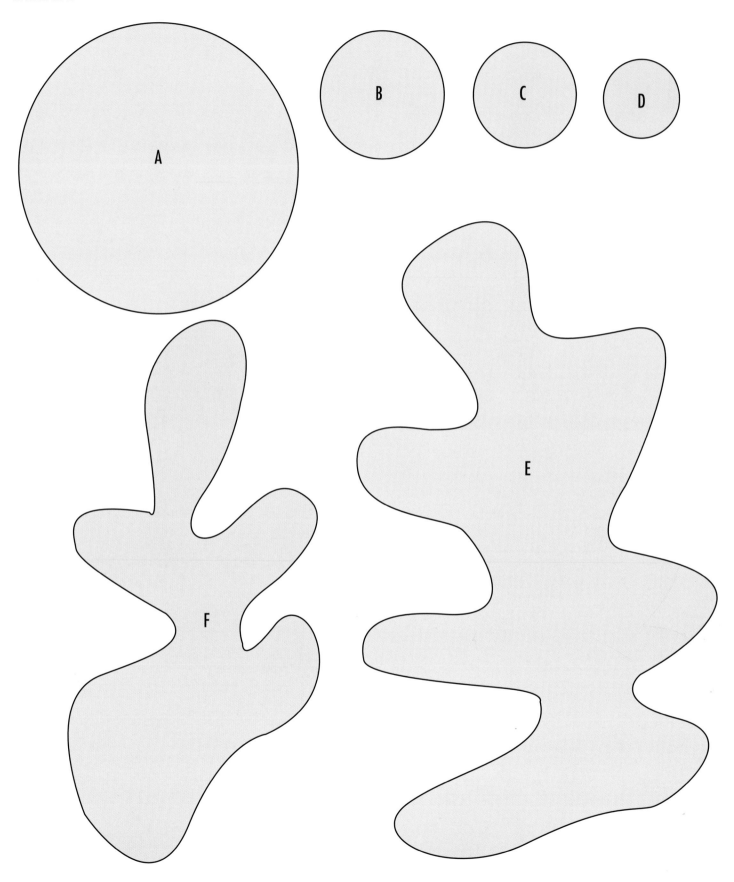

G

Enlarge 145%

I

Enlarge 145%

J

Enlarge 145%

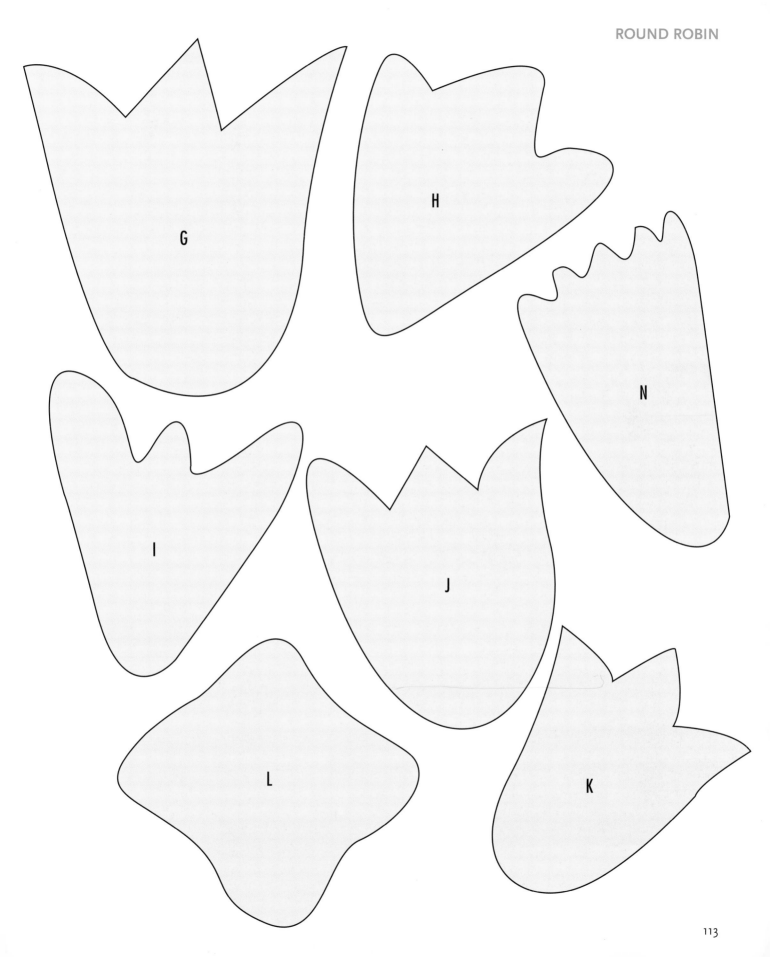

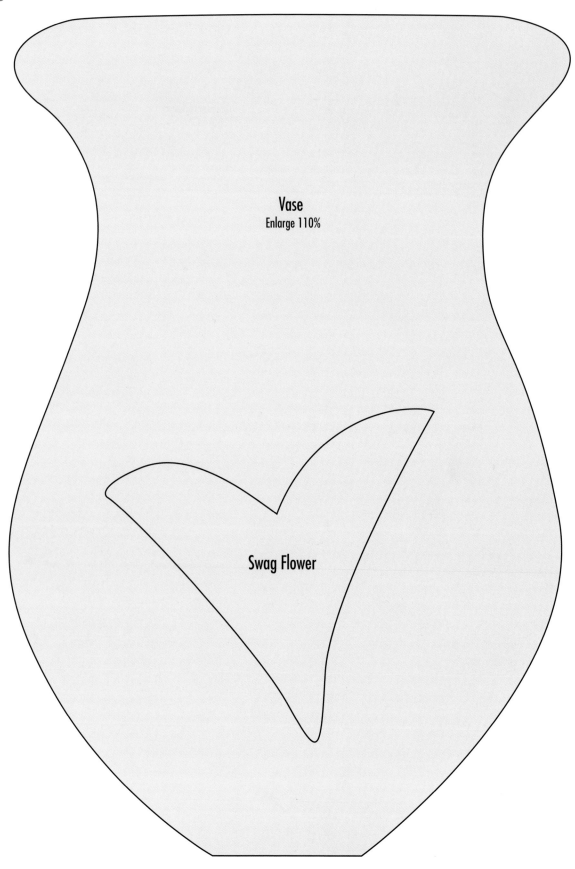

Vase
Enlarge 110%

Swag Flower

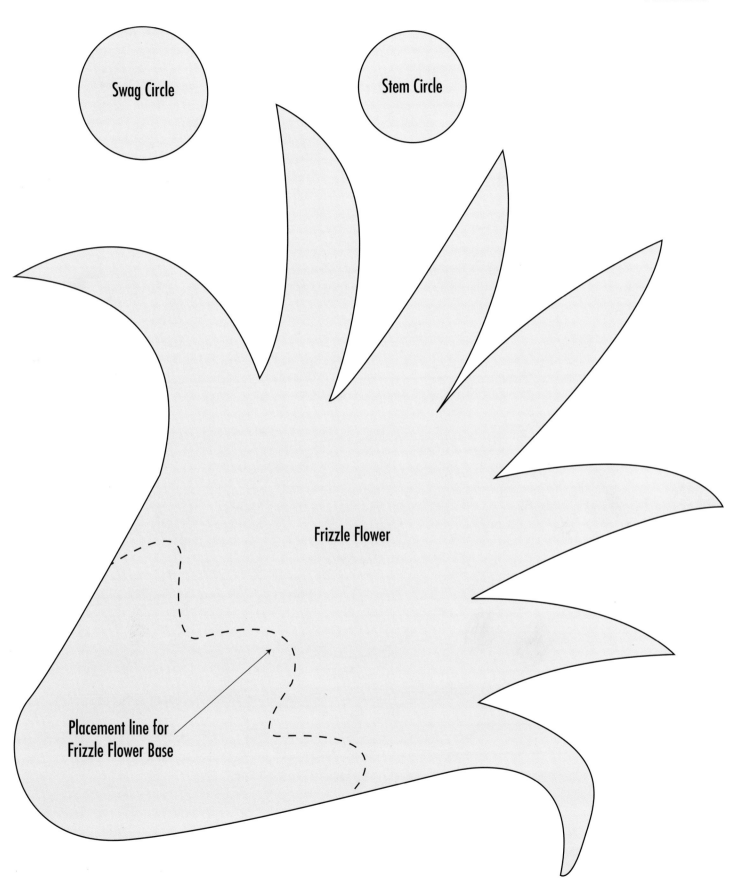

Swag Circle

Stem Circle

Frizzle Flower

Placement line for
Frizzle Flower Base

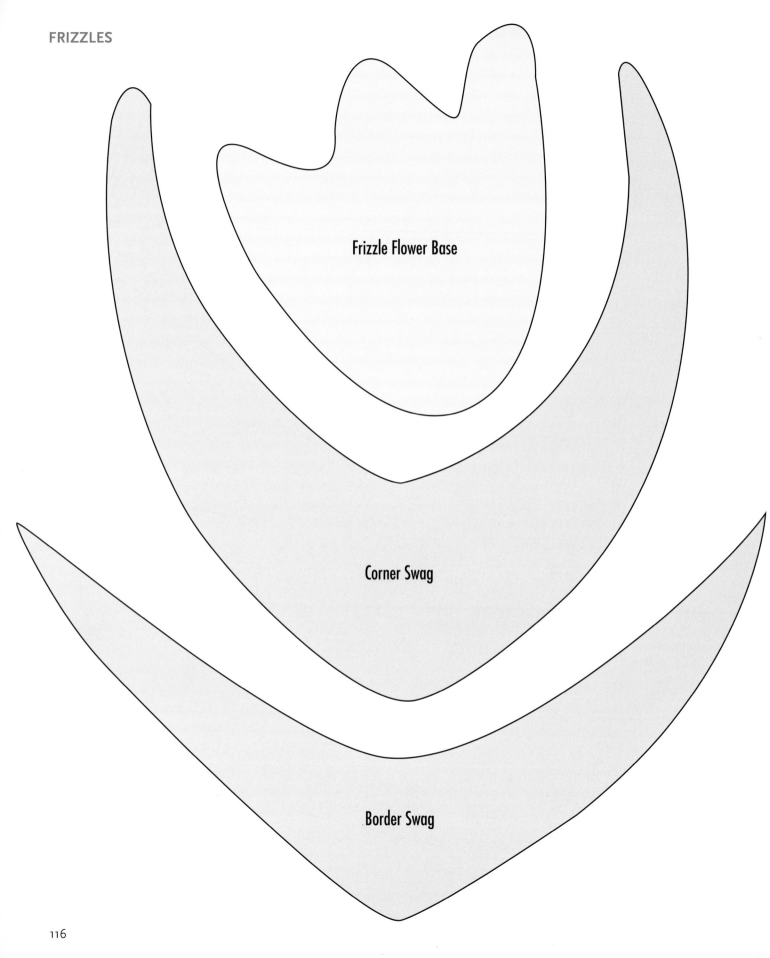

Frizzle Flower Base

Corner Swag

Border Swag

Vase

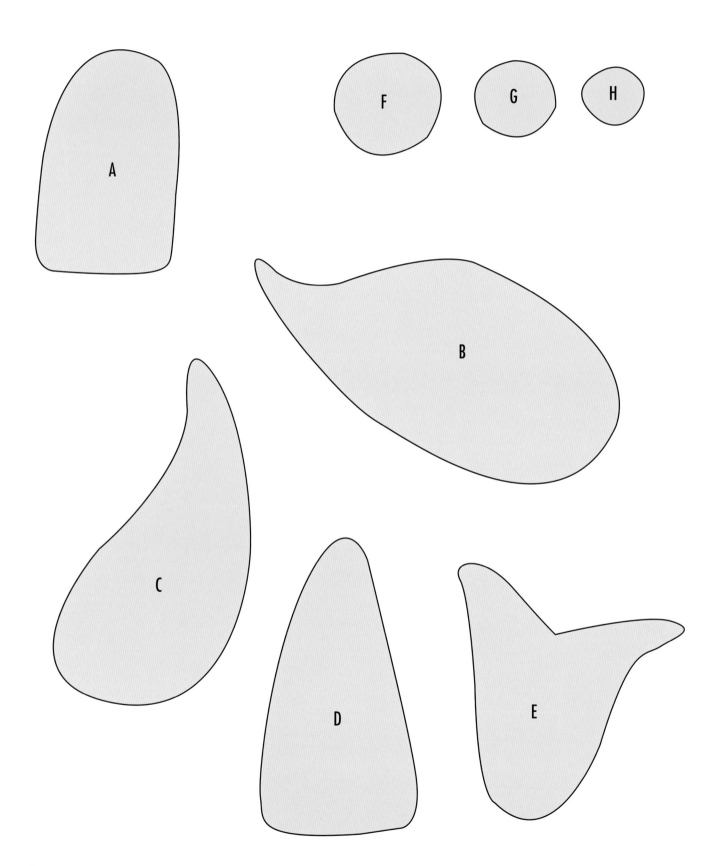

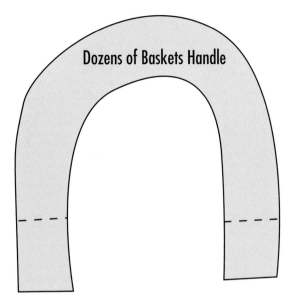

Dozens of Baskets Handle

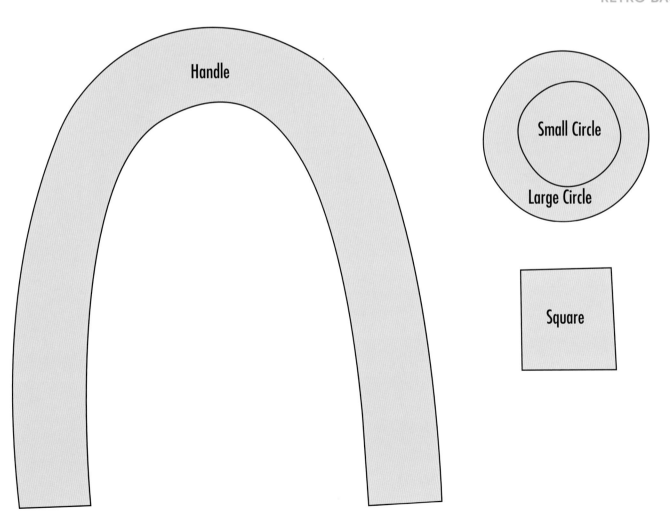

Handle

Small Circle

Large Circle

Square

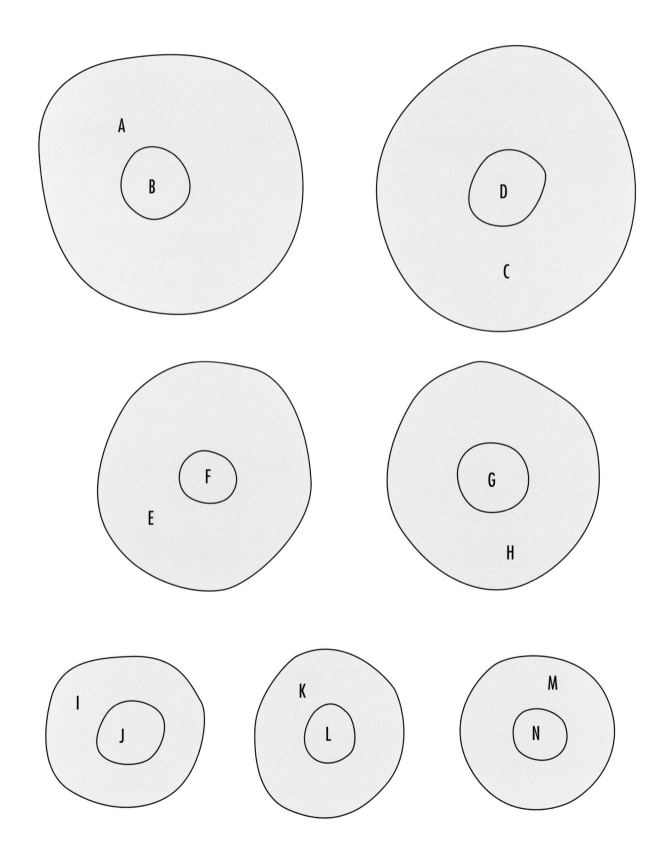

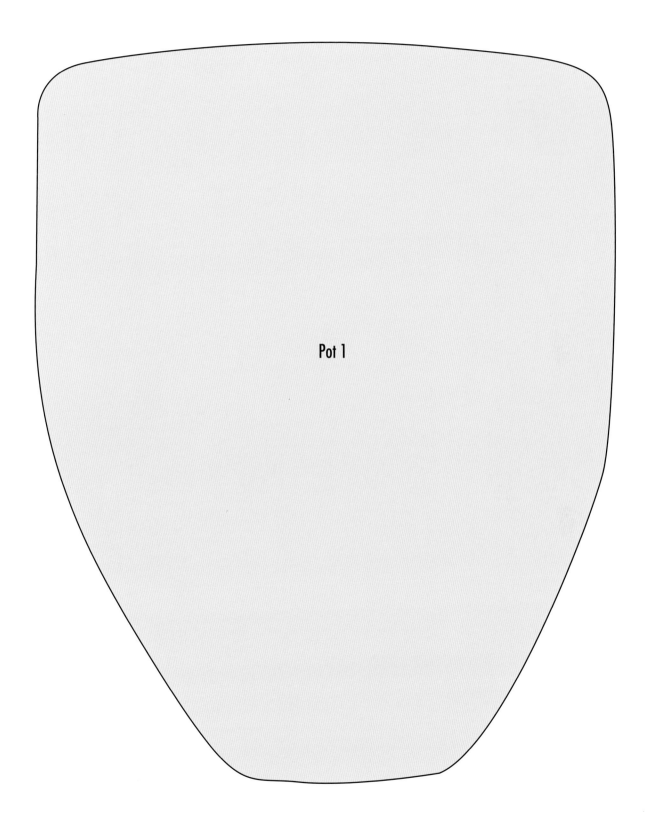

Pot 1

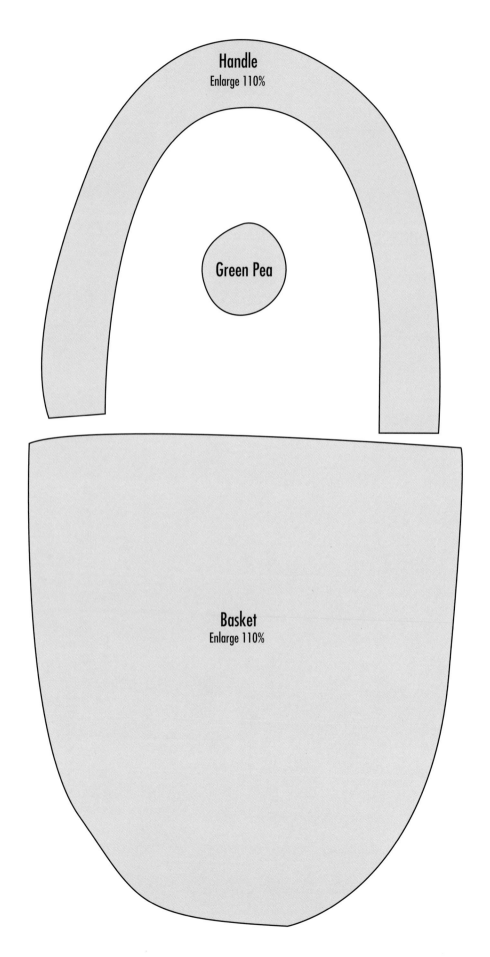

Handle
Enlarge 110%

Green Pea

Basket
Enlarge 110%

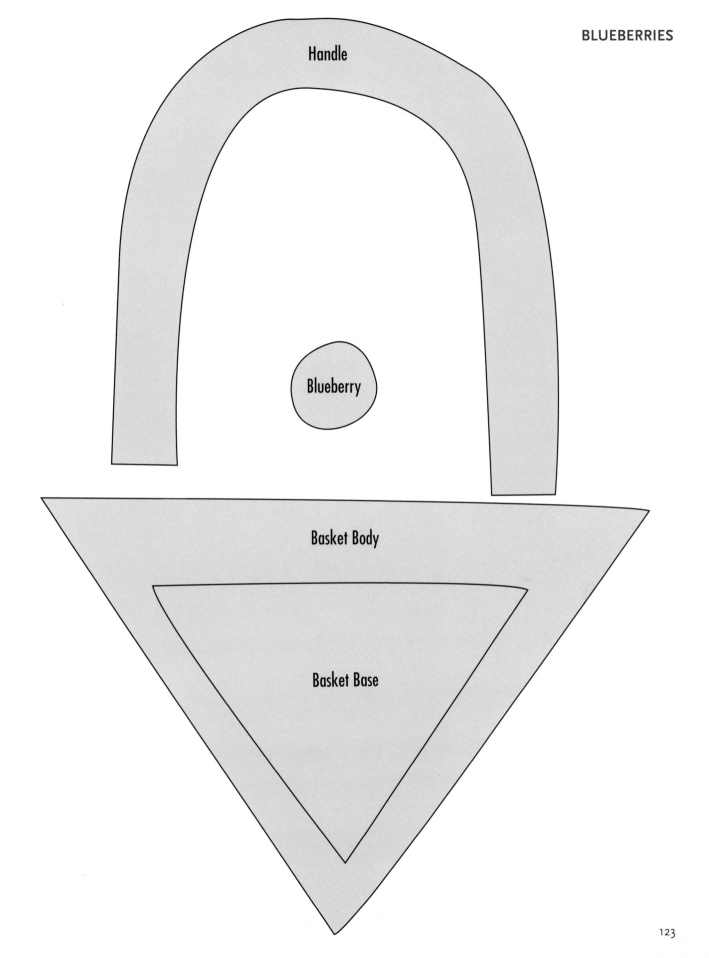

Handle

Blueberry

Basket Body

Basket Base

About the Author

Tonye Belinda Phillips has lived in the charming and picturesque mountain community of Camp Sherman, Oregon, for more than 35 years. She lives there with her husband, Doug, and their two teenage boys, Ande and Charlie. They enjoy an active and creative lifestyle that includes skiing, snowboarding, climbing, hiking, biking, sailing, and gardening.

After many years of knitting, embroidery, and cross-stitch, Tonye discovered quilting in 1992. She quickly fell in love with hand appliqué and hand quilting. Tonye teaches an occasional quilting or knitting class at The Stitchin' Post in Sisters, Oregon, and her work has been featured in several publications including *Transitions* by Andrea Balosky, *Through the Garden Gate* by Jean and Valori Wells, and *Quilted Memories* by Mary Lou Weidman. To see more of Tonye's work, visit www.tonyebelindaphillips.com.

Acknowledgments

Thank you to Jean Wells Keenan. Had it not been for the incredible amount of support and encouragement from you my dear friend, I am sure there would be no book. You are a truly amazing woman; always helpful and accommodating with friends, students, and even total strangers.

A special thank you to my loving sister, Donna Simpson, who has spent countless hours, days, and weeks trying to get me up to snuff in the technical department. You get the prize for the most patient and understanding person in the world.

Thank you to Andrea Balosky, a true artist and friend in every sense of the word. You helped me immensely with my transition to independent quilt maker.

Thanks to the Pine Needlers, my wonderful little quilt group in Camp Sherman. We have worked through a lot of laughs, tears, and fears over the years and I wouldn't change one bit of the experience. Also thanks to my Stitchin' Post "family," who has been friendly and supportive in every way.

To Kathy Deggendorfer, my studio neighbor and collaborator extraordinaire. Your paintings make me smile and you make me laugh out loud. And to Gwen Marston—how I love your style. You have given me much-needed encouragement and oodles of inspiration. And you are so funny!

To the Maui Babes, Gert, Kathy, Kitzie, Melinda, and Libby—Mahalo Title Babes!

Thanks Eileen Paulin, Rebecca Ittner, Catherine Risling, Darra Williamson and Rose Wright for taking me on, and thank you to "famous craft book photographer" Zac Williams. We have had some fun amongst the challenges.

Living in the Sisters, Oregon area has been a real pleasure. Not only is the natural beauty of the area absolutely stunning, but the people who live, work, and play here are incredibly creative. It is in the air everywhere. There are so many friends who have inspired and helped me along the way. I thank you all.

Index

Metric Equivalency Chart

mm-millimeters   cm-centimeters
inches to millimeters and centimeters

inches	mm	cm	inches	cm	inches	cm
1/8	3	0.3	9	22.9	30	76.2
1/4	6	0.6	10	25.4	31	78.7
1/2	13	1.3	12	30.5	33	83.8
5/8	16	1.6	13	33.0	34	86.4
3/4	19	1.9	14	35.6	35	88.9
7/8	22	2.2	15	38.1	36	91.4
1	25	2.5	16	40.6	37	94.0
1 1/4	32	3.2	17	43.2	38	96.5
1 1/2	38	3.8	18	45.7	39	99.1
1 3/4	44	4.4	19	48.3	40	101.6
2	51	5.1	20	50.8	41	104.1
2 1/2	64	6.4	21	53.3	42	106.7
3	76	7.6	22	55.9	43	109.2
3 1/2	89	8.9	23	58.4	44	111.8
4	102	10.2	24	61.0	45	114.3
4 1/2	114	11.4	25	63.5	46	116.8
5	127	12.7	26	66.0	47	119.4
6	152	15.2	27	68.6	48	121.9
7	178	17.8	28	71.1	49	124.5
8	203	20.3	29	73.7	50	127.0

yards to meters

yards	meters	yards	meters	yards	meters	yards	meters	yards	meters
1/8	0.11	2 1/8	1.94	4 1/8	3.77	6 1/8	5.60	8 1/8	7.43
1/4	0.23	2 1/4	2.06	4 1/4	3.89	6 1/4	5.72	8 1/4	7.54
3/8	0.34	2 3/8	2.17	4 3/8	4.00	6 3/8	5.83	8 3/8	7.66
1/2	0.46	2 1/2	2.29	4 1/2	4.11	6 1/2	5.94	8 1/2	7.77
5/8	0.57	2 5/8	2.40	4 5/8	4.23	6 5/8	6.06	8 5/8	7.89
3/4	0.69	2 3/4	2.51	4 3/4	4.34	6 3/4	6.17	8 3/4	8.00
7/8	0.80	2 7/8	2.63	4 7/8	4.46	6 7/8	6.29	8 7/8	8.12
1	0.91	3	2.74	5	4.57	7	6.40	9	8.23
1 1/8	1.03	3 1/8	2.86	5 1/8	4.69	7 1/8	6.52	9 1/8	8.34
1 1/4	1.14	3 1/4	2.97	5 1/4	4.80	7 1/4	6.63	9 1/4	8.46
1 3/8	1.26	3 3/8	3.09	5 3/8	4.91	7 3/8	6.74	9 3/8	8.57
1 1/2	1.37	3 1/2	3.20	5 1/2	5.03	7 1/2	6.86	9 1/2	8.69
1 5/8	1.49	3 5/8	3.31	5 5/8	5.14	7 5/8	6.97	9 5/8	8.80
1 3/4	1.60	3 3/4	3.43	5 3/4	5.26	7 3/4	7.09	9 3/4	8.92
1 7/8	1.71	3 7/8	3.54	5 7/8	5.37	7 7/8	7.20	9 7/8	9.03
2	1.83	4	3.66	6	5.49	8	7.32	10	9.14